VIEWPOINTS®
SERIES

Television

Other Books of Related Interest:

Opposing Viewpoints Series

Celebrity Culture

Children and the Entertainment Industry

Obesity

At Issue Series

Are Newspapers Becoming Extinct?

How Does Advertising Impact Teen Behavior?

Media Bias

Should Music Lyrics Be Censored?

Current Controversies Series

The Global Impact of Social Media

"Congress shall make no law . . . abridging the freedom of speech, or of the press."

First Amendment to the U.S. Constitution

The basic foundation of our democracy is the First Amendment guarantee of freedom of expression. The *Opposing Viewpoints* series is dedicated to the concept of this basic freedom and the idea that it is more important to practice it than to enshrine it.

OPPOSING
VIEWPOINTS®
SERIES

Television

Margaret Haerens, Book Editor

GREENHAVEN PRESS
A part of Gale, Cengage Learning

GALE
CENGAGE Learning™

Detroit • New York • San Francisco • New Haven, Conn • Waterville, Maine • London

GALE
CENGAGE Learning

Christine Nasso, *Publisher*
Elizabeth Des Chenes, *Managing Editor*

© 2011 Greenhaven Press, a part of Gale, Cengage Learning

Gale and Greenhaven Press are registered trademarks used herein under license.

For more information, contact:
Greenhaven Press
27500 Drake Rd.
Farmington Hills, MI 48331-3535
Or you can visit our Internet site at gale.cengage.com

For product information and technology assistance, contact us at

Gale Customer Support, 1-800-877-4253
For permission to use material from this text or product, submit all requests online at www.cengage.com/permissions

Further permissions questions can be emailed to permissionrequest@cengage.com

Articles in Greenhaven Press anthologies are often edited for length to meet page requirements. In addition, original titles of these works are changed to clearly present the main thesis and to explicitly indicate the author's opinion. Every effort is made to ensure that Greenhaven Press accurately reflects the original intent of the authors. Every effort has been made to trace the owners of copyrighted material.

Cover image copyright © iStockPhoto.com/Thanatham Piriyakamjanakul.

LIBRARY OF CONGRESS CATALOGING-IN-PUBLICATION DATA

Television / Margaret Haerens, book editor.
    p. cm. -- (Opposing viewpoints)
    Includes bibliographical references and index.
    ISBN 978-0-7377-5243-4 (hardcover) -- ISBN 978-0-7377-5244-1 (pbk.)
    1. Television broadcasting--Social aspects--Juvenile literature. I. Haerens, Margaret.
    PN1992.6.T3775 2011
    302.2'345--dc22
                                                    2010039232

Printed in the United States of America
1 2 3 4 5 6 7 15 14 13 12 11

Contents

Chapter 2: What Are the Issues of Reality Television?

Chapter 3: How Does Television Advertising Affect Society?

Chapter 4: How Should Television Be Regulated?

Why Consider
Opposing Viewpoints?

> "The only way in which a human being
> can make some approach to knowing the
> whole of a subject is by hearing what
> can be said about it by persons of every
> variety of opinion and studying all
> modes in which it can be looked at by
> every character of mind. No wise man
> ever acquired his wisdom in any mode
> but this."
>
> John Stuart Mill

In our media-intensive culture it is not difficult to find differing opinions. Thousands of newspapers and magazines and dozens of radio and television talk shows resound with differing points of view. The difficulty lies in deciding which opinion to agree with and which "experts" seem the most credible. The more inundated we become with differing opinions and claims, the more essential it is to hone critical reading and thinking skills to evaluate these ideas. Opposing Viewpoints books address this problem directly by presenting stimulating debates that can be used to enhance and teach these skills. The varied opinions contained in each book examine many different aspects of a single issue. While examining these conveniently edited opposing views, readers can develop critical thinking skills such as the ability to compare and contrast authors' credibility, facts, argumentation styles, use of persuasive techniques, and other stylistic tools. In short, the Opposing Viewpoints Series is an ideal way to attain the higher-level thinking and reading skills so essential in a culture of diverse and contradictory opinions.

In addition to providing a tool for critical thinking, *Opposing Viewpoints* books challenge readers to question their own strongly held opinions and assumptions. Most people form their opinions on the basis of upbringing, peer pressure, and personal, cultural, or professional bias. By reading carefully balanced opposing views, readers must directly confront new ideas as well as the opinions of those with whom they disagree. This is not to argue simplistically that everyone who reads opposing views will—or should—change his or her opinion. Instead, the series enhances readers' understanding of their own views by encouraging confrontation with opposing ideas. Careful examination of others' views can lead to the readers' understanding of the logical inconsistencies in their own opinions, perspective on why they hold an opinion, and the consideration of the possibility that their opinion requires further evaluation.

Evaluating Other Opinions

To ensure that this type of examination occurs, *Opposing Viewpoints* books present all types of opinions. Prominent spokespeople on different sides of each issue as well as well-known professionals from many disciplines challenge the reader. An additional goal of the series is to provide a forum for other, less known, or even unpopular viewpoints. The opinion of an ordinary person who has had to make the decision to cut off life support from a terminally ill relative, for example, may be just as valuable and provide just as much insight as a medical ethicist's professional opinion. The editors have two additional purposes in including these less known views. One, the editors encourage readers to respect others' opinions—even when not enhanced by professional credibility. It is only by reading or listening to and objectively evaluating others' ideas that one can determine whether they are worthy of consideration. Two, the inclusion of such viewpoints encourages the important critical thinking skill of objectively evaluating an author's credentials and bias. This evaluation will illuminate an author's reasons for taking a particular stance on an issue and will aid in readers' evaluation of the author's ideas.

It is our hope that these books will give readers a deeper understanding of the issues debated and an appreciation of the complexity of even seemingly simple issues when good and honest people disagree. This awareness is particularly important in a democratic society such as ours in which people enter into public debate to determine the common good. Those with whom one disagrees should not be regarded as enemies but rather as people whose views deserve careful examination and may shed light on one's own.

Thomas Jefferson once said that "difference of opinion leads to inquiry, and inquiry to truth." Jefferson, a broadly educated man, argued that "if a nation expects to be ignorant and free . . . it expects what never was and never will be." As individuals and as a nation, it is imperative that we consider the opinions of others and examine them with skill and discernment. The *Opposing Viewpoints* Series is intended to help readers achieve this goal.

David L. Bender and Bruno Leone,
Founders

Introduction

> *"Television is actually closer to reality than anything in books. The madness of TV is the madness of human life."*
>
> —*Camille Paglia,*
> *American social critic*

At the 2002 Billboard Music Awards, the singer Cher received the Artist Achievement award for her long success in the music industry. In her acceptance speech, which was broadcast live as it was happening, she stated: "People have been telling me I'm on the way out every year, right? So f--- them." Because it was live television, the expletive was not bleeped and was heard by millions of people.

A year later at the Billboard Music Awards, Nicole Ritchie was presenting an award to Paris Hilton, her friend and co-star in the reality show *The Simple Life*. "Have you ever tried to get cow shit out of a Prada purse?" Ritchie said on the live television show. "It's not so f-----g simple." Once again, censors were not able to bleep the curses in time, and they were broadcast to millions of viewers in primetime.

At the Golden Globe Awards show in 2003, Bono, the lead singer of U2, accepted an award for the band. In his acceptance speech, he exclaimed excitedly: "This is really, really f-----g brilliant." Because the ceremony was being broadcast live, the curse went out live, too.

After all three incidents, complaints flooded the networks and the offices of the Federal Communications Commission (FCC), which is in charge of overseeing and regulating network and cable television. In response to the avalanche of complaints, the FCC changed its policy in 2004 to state that fleeting expletives could be regarded actionably indecent and a finable offense. A fleeting expletive is a verbal profanity or visual obscenity uttered or shown during a live television or radio show, such as in the examples of Bono, Cher, and Nicole Ritchie. With their new policy, broadcasters would be fined up to $325,000 every time certain "patently offensive" expletives were aired. They also made clear that profanity referring to sex or excrement is always indecent and would be categorized as "patently offensive."

Immediately a challenge to the FCC's revised policy on fleeting expletives was issued by television networks NBC, ABC, CBS, and Fox. They claimed that the FCC failed to inform them of which words are "patently offensive" according to its policy. An appeals court determined that the FCC had violated federal law covering how agencies make regulations. In 2009, the US Supreme Court then reversed the decision of the appeals court, concluding that the FCC gave adequate explanation to comply with the law. They also sent the case back to the appeals court to reassess the indecency rules. As Justice Antonin Scalia wrote in his majority opinion on the case: "The commission could reasonably conclude that the pervasiveness of foul language, and the coarsening of public entertainment in other media such as cable, justify more stringent regulation of broadcast programs so as to give conscientious parents a relatively safe haven for their children."

In July 2010, however, the appeals court sided with the networks and ruled that the FCC's policy of regulating fleeting expletives is unconstitutionally vague. The court found that it is too difficult for networks to determine what is a finable offense from the policy and guidance given by the commission. The court also noted that while certain words were considered "patently offensive" and therefore finable, other similar expletives were not. As US Circuit Court of Appeals judge Rosemary Pooler wrote in the court's opinion on the case: "The FCC's policy violates the First Amendment because it is unconstitutionally vague, creating a chilling effect that goes far beyond the fleeting expletives at issue here." Pooler added that "by prohibiting all 'patently offensive' references to sex, sexual organs and excretion without giving adequate guidance as to what 'patently offensive' means, the FCC effectively chills speech, because broadcasters have no way of knowing what the FCC will find offensive."

The appeals court did leave the door open for the FCC by stating that the agency could craft a policy that would not violate the First Amendment and would also be clear enough for networks to fully understand the regulations and how they would be applied in practice.

The effect of fleeting expletives on American culture and the right of the FCC to regulate them illuminates issues of free speech and the government's role in defining what is acceptable and moral in society. While many argue that the government has a responsibility to monitor the airwaves and protect children from indecent language—even a fleeting expletive uttered during a live broadcast of a Hollywood awards show—others maintain that the right to free speech is important enough to endure a few curse words without society falling down around them.

The authors of the viewpoints presented in *Opposing Viewpoints: Television* debate many of these issues as well as others surrounding television and television advertising in the following chapters: What Values Does Television Promote? What Are the Issues of Reality Television? How Does Television Advertising Affect Society? and How Should Television Be Regulated?. The information in this volume will provide insight into the troubled relationship between the television networks and the FCC as well as the values television presents to millions of people in the United States and abroad.

OPPOSING
VIEWPOINTS®
SERIES

CHAPTER 1

What Values Does Television Promote?

Chapter Preface

It seems that in the beginning of every television season there is a deluge of commentary on the amount and quality of "family-friendly" programming on network television. Family-friendly programming includes dramas, reality television, and situation comedies that contain appropriate themes, content, and language for a broad family audience. These programs may touch on controversial themes, but they do so in a responsible manner and end with a morally responsible resolution. As media critic L. Brent Bozell III states in a 2008 *Human Events* article, family friendly "means what it plainly says—that you can put your grade-school children in front of it without wincing at bloody murders or needing a dictionary of sexual slang." In the past several years, there has been an influx of family-friendly networks on cable television that feature only wholesome programming. There are also organizations that monitor, rate, and recommend family-friendly programs, and there are awards shows that reward programs that feature morally responsible content.

Despite this emphasis on developing and supporting such programming, there are many media critics and cultural activists who believe that there are still not enough options for good, decent programming appropriate for families with children. These commentators assert that the majority of current shows still incorporate too much explicit and unsuitable sexual content, indecent language, and shocking scenes of violence to be truly good programming for discerning families. For these media critics, even shows touted as family friendly are often not.

Other commentators argue that there are an abundance of choices for families concerned about finding moral, wholesome television programs. They maintain that many television programs considered controversial or not family-friendly reflect the true nature of American society—with its gay and transgendered characters, violence, drug use, sexuality, and immoral choices—and should not be whitewashed as if the real world does not exist. For these commentators, protecting children does not mean hiding the way the world really is. Moreover, they question the standards by which advocates for family-friendly programming judge television programs, stating that what is immoral or offensive to one person may not be to another.

Another concern is that the debate over family-friendly television is just a way for one group to impose its religious, political, and/or moral values on another. Both sides of the issue believe that programming that presents one side of the cultural or political divide in a positive light to the exclusion of other viewpoints will have undue influence on children and families. In that way, the perennial haggling over the moral content of television programming is often considered a mask for a much broader cultural debate on religion, political ideology, and social mores.

The debate over the quality and amount of family-friendly programming is one that is explored in the following chapter, which examines the values that television promotes. Other issues discussed are gay stereotypes on television, whether torture is being encouraged, and whether television reflects society's values.

*"In the past, television did not look re-
alistically at the nuances of human behavior. Somebody was either all good
or all bad."*

Television Reflects
Societal Values

Anna Stewart

Anna Stewart is a reporter for Variety. *In the following viewpoint, she maintains that current television shows more accurately reflect the nuances and complexity of modern society than
in earlier generations. Stewart argues that these recent shows
hold a strong appeal for viewers because they allow them the opportunity to do such things as live vicariously through a serial
killer or feel like a cool insider in Hollywood.*

As you read, consider the following questions:

1. How does Dr. Drew Pinsky believe that television is
   catching up with American life, according to the author?

2. According to Stewart, what is the appeal of the television show *Entourage*?

3. Why does Pinsky, according to the author, believe television reflects a healthier attitude about ourselves?

How many people haven't had the urge to murder one or two bad guys. Sell some marijuana to make ends meet. Or behave like a bad boss. There's a little Dexter Morgan, Nancy Botwin and Jack Donaghy in everybody. Today, couch vigilantes get their kicks out of watching shows like *Dexter*, *Weeds* and *30 Rock*, not to mention seven other WGA [Writers Guild of America] nommed [nominated] TV shows.

TV Is More Nuanced

"Television is catching up with American life in many ways," says Dr. Drew Pinsky of *Celebrity Rehab With Dr. Drew*. We are looking more realistically at our family structure and our pathology. Fifty years ago, the mirror that is television had us watching *The Flintstones* as a reflection of our family life. Now it's *The Simpsons*.

Dexter Morgan is the serial killer with charm. "People believe that the system has failed them," explains celebrity divorce attorney Raoul Felder, "and they're hailing somebody who takes the law into his own hands. He's like [actor] Charles Bronson in *Death Wish* and people are cheering."

"People are looking to vent," adds TV shrink "Dr. Phil" McGraw. "It's a safe outlet for them to live vicariously. They don't have to do anything bad. They don't have to sacrifice their morality. They can sit on their couches and quietly urge this guy on."

Weeds portrays both ends of the moral spectrum. "We have a widowed housewife on one end. Your heart goes out to her," Felder observes, "and, at the other end of the spectrum, she's a marijuana dealer. From illegality to conventional tragedy, there's a lot to be sympathetic about."

Shows Reflect Society

When people look back at the 2000's, they're also going to remember *Lost, Mad Men* and *Friday Night Lights* and muse about our cultural evolution.

"These are the programs that engrossed the people," says [online video service] Revision3 executive Ron Richards. "*Lost* is people that you can relate to: It's a doctor, it's a thug guy, it's a fat guy. It's people who reflect our society. The show really tickles the desire or hope for something exciting to happen in their lives. Nobody wants to be stranded on an island in the South Pacific and have horrible things happen to them, but for an hour it's fun to go there."

"I think audiences expect a level of depth that they didn't when there were just only three television networks," says *Diggnation's* David Prager. "Younger generations of storytellers are having to cope with audiences that are interested in being impressed by a level of depth."

The In-Crowd

Entourage touches upon our fascination with celebrity. Everybody wants to be in the cool kids club, and the show gives us entree.

"There's a lot to attract people," Felder says. "You see what's going on behind the camera. It then makes you feel that celebrities have feet of clay, too. Makes you feel good when you watch it."

What accounts for some of *30 Rock's* success is its nudge-nudge, wink-wink that is really *Saturday Night Live.*

"To set *30 Rock* behind the scenes of a show that we have known and loved for years, a show that has been the center of cool, is to build a base that people can relate to," Richards says. "It's building off, hey, this cool environment that we would love to be part of, and now *30 Rock* is letting us do that."

Sophisticated Viewers

Nearly countless cable channels, plus the Internet, have made even children very savvy viewers.

"We've sophisticated our audience up so many ratchets," McGraw says. "*The Partridge Family* simply would not work today because there's knowledge and awareness. And for television to work, it has to be relevant. When we see Homer Simpson act out with Bart, I think everybody knows that's a characterization of what parents feel; that's why it resonates."

In the past, television did not look realistically at the nuances of human behavior. Somebody was either all good or all bad.

"We have become more accepting of who we really are, rather than trying to be someone we are not," Pinsky says. "We look at ourselves and say, 'We're OK.' I think it's reflective of healthier attitudes. And, rather than insisting on a one-dimensional, propagandistic version of what we're supposed to be, we're accepting of a broad range of the human experience in the American media. It's healthy.

"The character in *Weeds* is so sick, but I love her. I really appreciate the human struggle that this woman has. And *Dexter* is a good example of the fact that people who do really bad things really only do them under certain circumstances. Not everyone is an ax murderer all the time."

> *"Americans know that there is a big dif-*
> *ference between U.S. pop culture and*
> *the way they actually live. But most*
> *foreigners don't."*

Television Does Not Accurately Reflect Societal Values

Dinesh D'Souza

Dinesh D'Souza is an author, public speaker, and contributor to the Christian Science Monitor *and other publications. In the following viewpoint, D'Souza discusses the view foreign countries have of Americans. He claims that while the Europeans empha-size the "shoot-first, ask-questions-later" attitude of America, Muslims emphasize Americans' family breakdown and vulgar popular culture. D'Souza contends that the anti-Americanism is focusing only on one side of America and although Americans know they live differently than they are portrayed on television and in popular culture, foreigners are only exposed to the America that is shown on television and in movies.*

Dinesh D'Souza, "War on Terror's Other Front: Cleaning Up U.S. Pop Culture," *Christian Science Monitor*, January 25, 2007. Reproduced by permission.

As you read, consider the following questions:

1. What does D'Souza claim the Muslims view as the "'horrors' of 'blue' America"?

2. What does the author say is a key reason that Muslims "focus their anger on the United States"?

3. What play does D'Souza reference in the article for its "in-your-face" material?

Anti-Americanism comes in different varieties. The European kind emphasizes the "evils" of "red" America: a shoot-first, ask-questions-later cowboy in the White House, and Bible-toting fundamentalists walking around the corridors of power.

The Muslim variety is very different. Many Muslims point to the "horrors" of "blue" America: homosexual marriage, family breakdown, and a popular culture that is trivial, materialistic, vulgar, and, in many cases, morally repulsive.

This latter view is dangerously—and justifiably—common in many traditional cultures across the globe. Because it feeds their perception that American values are inimical to their way of life, this attitude can blossom into the kind of anti-American pathology that partly fueled the 9/11 attacks. Any serious effort to shore up America's security must include steps to edify American culture.

Reacting to a Distorted Projection

Both the European and Muslim brands of anti-Americanism, of course, are focused on only one side of America. They are reacting not so much to America per se as to the often distorted projections of U.S. policy and culture across the globe. Americans know that there is a big difference between U.S. pop culture and the way they actually live. But most foreigners don't. The America they see in movies and on television is often the only one they know.

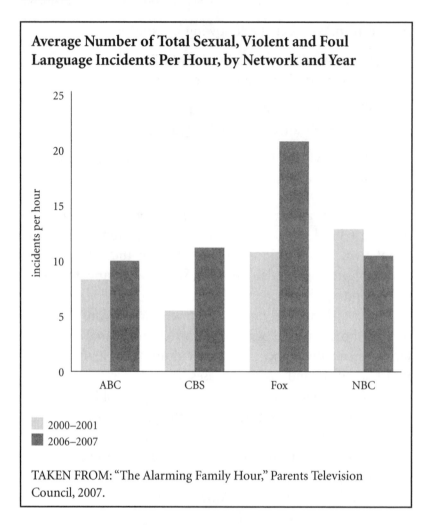

Average Number of Total Sexual, Violent and Foul Language Incidents Per Hour, by Network and Year

incidents per hour

- 2000–2001
- 2006–2007

TAKEN FROM: "The Alarming Family Hour," Parents Television Council, 2007.

Critics of globalization complain that the U.S. is corrupting the world with its multinational corporations and its trade practices. But surveys such as the Pew Research Center studies of world opinion show that non-Western peoples are generally pleased with American products.

In fact, the people of Asia, Africa, and the Middle East want more American companies, more American technology, and more free trade. Their objection is not to McDonald's or Microsoft but to America's cultural values.

These sentiments are felt very keenly in the Muslim world. As an Iranian from Neishapour told journalist Afshin Molavi, "People say we want freedom. You know what these foreign-inspired people want? They want the freedom to gamble and drink and bring vice to our Muslim land. This is the kind of freedom they want."

Muslim critics of American culture are quick to concede its fascination and attraction, especially to the young. Some time ago, I saw an interview with a Muslim sheikh on TV. The interviewer told the sheikh, "I find it curious and hypocritical that you are so anti-American, considering that two of your sons are living and studying in America."

The sheikh replied, "But this is not hypocritical at all. I concede that American culture is appealing. If you put a young man into a hotel room and give him dozens of pornography tapes, he is likely to find those appealing as well. What America appeals to is everything that is low and disgusting in human nature."

The most powerful of all the American offenses recited in the lands of Islam, argues preeminent Middle East expert Bernard Lewis, "is the degeneracy and debauchery of the American way of life."

A major reason why some Muslims focus their anger on the United States is because it is American culture—not Swedish culture or French culture—that is finding its way into every nook and cranny of Islamic society.

Cultural Blowback

There is a cultural blowback against America that is coming from all the traditional cultures of Africa, South America, the Middle East, and Asia. This resistance is summed up in a slogan used by Singapore's former prime minister, Lee Kuan Yew: "Modernization without Westernization." What this means is that traditional cultures want prosperity and technology, but they don't want the values of American culture.

The Islamic radicals are the most extreme and politically mobilized segment of this global resistance, and they are recruiting innumerable ordinary Muslims to their proclaimed jihad against the values America represents. The radicals have been remarkably successful in convincing traditional Muslims that America represents a serious threat to the Islamic religion.

In one of his post-9/11 propaganda videos, [terrorist leader] Osama bin Laden said that Islam faces the greatest threat it has faced since the time of Muhammad. How could he possibly think this? Not because of US troops that were in Saudi Arabia. Not even because of Israel. The threat bin Laden is referring to is an infiltration of American values and mores into the lives of Muslims, transforming their society and destroying their traditional values and religious beliefs.

Even the term "Great Satan," so commonly used to denounce America in the Muslim world, is better understood when we recall that in the traditional understanding, shared by Judaism, Christianity, and Islam, Satan is not a conqueror; he is a tempter. In one of its best-known verses, the Koran describes Satan as "the insidious tempter who whispers into the hearts of men."

Are the Radical Muslims Right?

These concerns prompt a startling thought: Are the radical Muslims right? Surely, some American parents can at least sympathize. Consider the profane language on prime-time TV, or the salacious themes so prevalent in movies and music. Need I even mention the vulgarity of some rap lyrics, or the Jerry Springer and Howard Stern shows?

The Muslim indictment extends to "high culture," to liberal culture that offers itself as refined and sophisticated. In America, Eve Ensler's play, "The Vagina Monologues," has won rave reviews and generated a pop culture phenomenon. But if its in-your-face focus on female genitalia makes some Americans uncomfortable, just imagine the reaction the performance and accompanying book is getting abroad, in places such as China, Turkey, Pakistan, and Egypt. Can foreigners be blamed for feeling defiled by this American export?

To many American liberals, pop culture reflects the values of individuality, personal autonomy, and freedom of expression. Thus, it is seen as a moral achievement. But viewed from the perspective of people in the traditional societies of the world, notably the Muslim world, these same trends appear to be nothing less than the shameless promotion of depravity.

So it is not surprising to see pious Muslims react with horror at the prospect of this new American morality seeping into their part of the world. They rightly fear that this new morality will destroy their religion and way of life.

So what should America do about this? First, it must recognize the global implications of the culture wars. Indeed the culture war and the war on terror are linked. The restoration of America's culture will be a moral boost to its children—and it will help the nation's image abroad.

As a practical matter, of course, such a cultural restoration will not be easy. At the very least, it is a task that will take decades.

Show the World America's "Good" Side

The best we Americans can do is to show Muslims, and traditional people around the world, the "other America" that they often don't see. [President George W.] Bush and his administration spokespersons should in their speeches do more to highlight the values of conservative and religious America. They should not be afraid to speak out against American cultural exports that are shameless and corrupting.

Moreover, we should do what we can to stop the export of debased American values abroad. In the United Nations, for example, America should work with Muslims, Hindus, Buddhists, and others to block the efforts of leftist groups around the world who promote radical feminism, homosexuality, prostitution, and pornography as "rights" under international law. Instead, the US should align itself with social decency and traditional family values.

As citizens, we should not hesitate to tell traditional Muslims and others that there are many of us who are working to reverse the tide of cultural depravity in our society and around the world.

By proclaiming our allegiance to the traditional values of Judeo-Christian society, we can reduce the currents of anti-Americanism among the Muslims, and thus undercut the appeal of radical Islam to traditional Muslims around the world.

"America is in the throes of a raging de-
cency epidemic."

Television Offers Programs with Family-Friendly Values

Greg Beato

Greg Beato is a contributor to a number of publications, includ-
ing Reason, Wired, *and the* San Francisco Chronicle. *In the fol-*
lowing viewpoint, he asserts that Hollywood is producing a vari-
ety of family-friendly television programming. Beato argues that
the Parents Television Council, a conservative group that moni-
tors television, frequently exaggerates the violence and swearing
in programs in order to make the threat more dire than it is.

As you read, consider the following questions:

1. What are the CAMIEs, according to Beato?

2. According to the author, how many of the twenty movies that got the widest circulation in 2007 were rated R?

3. According to Beato, what does the Parents Television
Council employ lip readers for?

Greg Beato, "Hollywood's Decency Epidemic," *Reason*, May 2008. Copyright © 2008 by
Reason. Reproduced by permission.

On May 3, [2008,] at the Wilshire Theater in Beverly Hills, there won't be a single shamelessly naked trophy in the house. The 2008 CAMIE Awards will be celebrating "Character And Morality In Entertainment," and in contrast to the disturbingly androgynous and probably bisexual Oscar [Academy Award statuette], the CAMIE statuette is clad in a wholesome dress that leaves everything to the imagination except a beguiling flash of patinated bronze ankle. But don't be getting any ideas, fresh guy! According to CAMIE's creators, she is "a lovely and modest young woman."

The CAMIEs

While Hollywood is the Thomas Edison of self-congratulation, always inventing new ways to honor itself, Tinseltown is apparently too busy churning out simulated sex and lovingly choreographed gore to devise an awards show that emphasizes family-friendly entertainment. Thus, the task was left to outsiders, and in 2001 Dr. Glen Griffin, a retired pediatrician and abstinence advocate from Salt Lake City, [Utah,] organized the first CAMIEs. The event was held at lunchtime, in a local park, and it seems safe to say that whatever its attractions were, [actress] Gwyneth Paltrow in a see-thru Alexander McQueen mesh tank-top was not one of them.

In 2005 the CAMIE Awards migrated to Los Angeles, and the production has been growing quickly ever since. Each year, it honors five theatrical and five made-for-TV movies that feature "positive role models who build character, overcome adversity, correct unwise choices, strengthen families, live moral lives and solve life's problems with integrity and perseverance." And each year, more and more industry types show up to pay tribute to technicolor virtue and inoffensiveness. "The reception from Hollywood has been great," exclaims CAMIE Awards Productions president Joseph Lake.

Wait, Hollywood? The same Hollywood that presidential candidate Barack Obama recently chastised for allegedly marketing "violent, slasher, horror films" to six-year-olds? The same Hollywood that the Senate's own [film critics] Siskel and Ebert, [US senators] John McCain and Hillary Clinton, have been panning for years now, via testy congressional hearings and proposals like the "Media Marketing Accountability Act"? (That would have made it potentially illegal to market R-rated movies in any medium with children under 17 in the audience.) The same Hollywood that packs TV's "family hour" with 4.19 violent incidents, 3.76 sexual references or situations, 0.01 bleeped "cocksuckers," and 1.08 unbleeped "hells" per hour in a wicked attempt to poison the minds of innocent and impressionable Parents Television Council employees?

A Decency Epidemic

Look around. America is in the throes of a raging decency epidemic. On *American Idol*, TV's perennial ratings champ, even the edgiest contestants are a temporary-tattoo-removal away from blending in at an Osmond Family [a wholesome music group] reunion. Reigning Disney Channel poppet Miley Cyrus oozes 100-proof adorableness so relentlessly that one suspects she actually has tiny little paws instead of hands and feet. The casts of tween favorites like *Zoey 101* and *High School Musical* are so wholesome they make those hoodlums from *Saved by the Bell* look like extras in a [director and producer Martin] Scorsese film.

Of the 20 movies that got the widest circulation in 2007, only two were rated R. From 2005 to 2007, during the traditional summer movie season—the first weekend of May through Labor Day—only 40 R-rated movies and zero NC-17 movies opened up in 500 or more theaters. According to the box office tracking firm Exhibitor Relations, this represents just 29 percent of movies in wide release.

In September 2006, Fox established a stand-alone division called Fox Faith to distribute movies with strong Christian themes. It also partnered with Walden Media—the production company created by billionaire Phillip Anschutz that has developed such hits as *Charlotte's Web, Bridge to Terabithia,* and *The Lion, the Witch, and the Wardrobe*—with the aim of producing a half-dozen family-friendly movies a year.

Finding Interest in Unlikely Places

Even Hollywood's bad boys are going soft. During their tenure at Miramax, Harvey and Bob Weinstein released movies like *Priest, Kids,* and *Dogma,* and were only slightly less reviled than gay marriage amongst the family values brigade. At their new gig, the Weinstein Company, they've signed a multi-year first-look deal with Impact Entertainment, a Christian production company.

"Studios who in the past weren't even interested in talking to us about this kind of stuff are submitting products to us on a regular basis," says the CAMIEs' Joseph Lake. "This year, we could have picked 20 movies to honor. Or even more—there were that many really good ones." The Dove Foundation, a nonprofit organization that encourages the "production, distribution and consumption of wholesome family entertainment," issued its blue-and-white "Family-Approved Seal" to 58 feature films released in 2007.

For connoisseurs of tasteful A-list nudity and deftly emoted expletives, things are getting a little dire. If you want to seamlessly exterminate the coarse language, blood-soaked imagery, and sexual themes from R-rated titles like *The Texas Chainsaw Massacre* and *Lethal Weapon 4* so you can more comfortably consume their more positive, character-building messages with your family in a safe viewing environment, there is a device, the ClearPlay DVD player, that promises to do just this. But where is the machine that can make the excruciatingly dainty *Miss Potter* more engaging by magically deleting [actress] Renee Zellweger's Victorian bodice on occasion, or inserting a charming explosion or two?

Desperate to Find Fault

Alas, even as the floodtides of rectitude threaten to give us all a cleansing soak, the Culture War's most dogged mercenaries grow increasingly desperate to sound notes of alarm. The Parents Television Council is so eager to characterize your flat-screen as the portal to Satan's eternal multiplex that it actually characterizes the plastic surgeries on the MTV show *I Want a New Face* as "violent incidents." It also employs eagle-eyed lip-readers to decipher and categorize the bleeped-out utterances of reality TV contestants. In 180 hours of family-hour programming the group recently assessed, there were 30 bleeped "f---"s, one bleeped "bitch," one bleeped "asshole," and an especially troubling 54 "unknown" bleeps.

In a column touting the October 2007 release of the animated movie *The Ten Commandments*, the conservative pundit Janice Shaw Crouse noted that only two of the top 20 grossing movies of 2005 had an R rating. "This shift in public tastes has yet to be recognized by the Hollywood elites, who continue to promote movies that are less financially successful at the box office," she concluded, without bothering to reveal the mysterious entity that created, distributed, and marketed the other 18. Has Lincoln, Nebraska, suddenly turned into a hotbed of major studio film production?

At this point, there is pretty much too much content for everyone—you can waste your entire life watching warm, gentle tales of perseverance and uplift just as easily as you can waste it watching hardcore porn. While the Internet has shown us that Hollywood will never out-sleaze a Wichita housewife with a members-only website, or out-mayhem the grassroots auteurs behind *Ghetto Fights #3*, the Industry does its best to keep pace. It regularly convinces dewy ingenues like [actresses] Natalie Portman and Anne Hathaway that they will not be taken seriously as artists until they prove their nipples can act too. It gives [actor] Sylvester Stallone $50 million to see how many decapitations he can simulate in 91 minutes. And that's exactly why so many of us will always love Hollywood.

A Myriad of Choices

But the choice is no longer between frontal nudity and disembodied heads. When the aforementioned *Ten Commandments* opened on 830 screens yet ended up grossing less than $1 million in its four-week run, it was actually great news for decency advocates. Apparently there is so much wholesome programming out there that the audience for such stuff can afford to be a little choosy.

Nor did *The Ten Commandments* make the CAMIE Awards cut, either. Which, if you think about it, is a fairly stunning development. A bunch of family-friendly outsiders from Salt Lake City have deemed the work of traditional Hollywood elites like 20th Century Fox and Warner Bros. more uplifting than a film based on the Bible itself.

> "[Family-friendly programming] should mean what it plainly says—that you can put your grade-school children in front of it without wincing at bloody murders or needing a dictionary of sexual slang."

Television Does Not Offer Enough Family-Friendly Programs

L. Brent Bozell III

L. Brent Bozell III is the president of the Media Research Center. In the following viewpoint, he contends that the definition of "family-friendly" has been watered down to the point that programs considered family-friendly are not. Bozell points to Heroes *and* Ugly Betty *as two shows recently recognized as family-friendly, but are filled with violence and sexual references.*

As you read, consider the following questions:

1. According to Bozell, what did one television critic say about the Family Friendly Programming Forum Awards?

L. Brent Bozell III, "What Does 'Family Friendly' Mean?" *Human Events*, January 3, 2008. Copyright © 2008 by Human Events. Reproduced by permission.

2. How many instances of sexual content did the Parents Television Council (PTC) count in the first season of *Ugly Betty*, according to the author?

3. How many examples of foul language did the PTC count in the first season of *Ugly Betty*, according to Bozell?

It was encouraging, almost a decade ago, when it was announced that some corporate advertisers had banded together to offer their corporate support for television shows that were more friendly to viewing by entire families. The group was called the Family Friendly Programming Forum [FFPF], and over the years, its presence certainly has helped bring some safer programming to television.

But in the world of the networks, where sleaze, sex, blood and shock are the rule, the definition of "family friendly" can easily be watered down—and has been. One TV critic announced the FFPF's annual awards show on the CW network in a logical way: "With all the innuendo and violence in primetime shows, it's amazing they can even field a group of nominees for the annual Family Television Awards."

Take a Look at the Winners

Forget the trouble with fielding nominees. Ask yourself: What about the winners? The FFPF's top award-winning "family friendly" shows were NBC's *Heroes* for best drama and ABC's *Ugly Betty* for best comedy.

Just how "family friendly" are these shows?

Heroes, an action comic book that came to life, presented a compelling first season around the concept that everyday people who discovered they had superpowers were suddenly threatened with an evil conspiracy to eliminate their gifted kind. It isn't as "corny" as a classic comic book. While its good and evil characters are assembled to root for and against, some heroes are "complex," that Hollywood euphemism for

bizarre. Take, for example, the schizophrenic mother whose "super" alter ego is only heroic in that she will kill anyone who endangers her child.

Heroes is also a show with plenty of dark themes and violence. Its primary villain, named Sylar, has a nasty habit of slicing the tops of heads off of his victims. As the season drew to a close, another villain succumbed when a mortally wounded hero put a fist-sized hole in his skull. The whole season was predicated on one of the central heroes fearing that he would cause the mass murder of New York with the wrongful application of his powers. For young children, NBC could have easily called this show *Nightmares.*

Ugly Betty Is Even Worse

But *Ugly Betty* was an even less acceptable choice because it was presented to FFPF and ABC before it ever aired as a "family friendly" alternative. The title character is Betty Suarez, a sympathetic Mexican American secretary at a fashion magazine cursed with ugly glasses, braces and zero fashion sense. After the loss of her mother, Betty is clearly the glue that holds her family together: her father, her adult sister and a nephew. She also helps keep her fashion-magazine boss, a natural playboy, on a straighter and narrower path. She's a nerdy heroine in a morally upside-down world.

But anyone watching this show's first season could see that the "family friendly" tag just doesn't apply anywhere near this.

The Parents Television Council's analysts counted 205 instances of sexual content and 154 examples of foul language in just the first season. They also found catty references to oral sex, genital size, pornography, strippers, anal sex, threesomes, kinky and fetishistic behavior, transsexuals, statutory rape, sadism, and masochism.

With this show set in the fashion industry, the show is heavy on sexual scenes and sex talk, straight and gay. *Ugly Betty* has several gay characters and a transgendered former man (improbably played by former supermodel Rebecca Romijn). Even Betty's teenaged nephew, Justin, is effeminate and loves the fashion industry. They've never openly addressed whether he is gay, but the show's creator, Silvio Horta, is gay and said the Justin character will experience "the journey" as he matures on the show. "I see myself in him," Horta says. The actor playing Justin is 12, but Horta loves the way he is "able to play up the flamboyance."

Too Many Sexual References

The writers love to throw gay and lesbian references in everywhere. In a recent show, guest star Betty White, playing herself, declared that she adored her fans, "except for the few sickos who write lesbian fan fiction about me and [fellow *Golden Girls* actress] Bea Arthur."

This is "family friendly"? When a show can win both a Family Television Award and a Media Award from the Gay and Lesbian Alliance Against Defamation [GLAAD], as *Ugly Betty* has, you know there's something wrong. With a pile of plots advancing the gay agenda, a GLAAD Award is appropriate. A "family friendly" award is insulting.

What does the FFPF think the phrase "family friendly" means? It shouldn't just mean a show with sympathetic leading characters. It should mean what it plainly says—that you can put your grade-school children in front of it without wincing at bloody murders or needing a dictionary of sexual slang. These choices make you wonder if that TV critic is right. Is network TV so far gone that *these* shows are the ones who most deserve awards for wholesomeness?

"There's so much more to the gay community than the people on TV (or at a gay-pride parade)."

Television Promotes Gay Stereotypes

Ramin Setoodeh

Ramin Setoodeh is a Newsweek *reporter. In the following viewpoint, he contends that the increasing number of gay characters on television has led to a proliferation of more stereotypically gay characters, which may be leading to a greater intolerance of gays. Setoodeh argues that these characters may have to exhibit more balance in order to be accepted in the mainstream.*

As you read, consider the following questions:

1. What does Setoodeh identify as an incident that "paved the way for gay characters of every stripe"?

2. How did voters in Maine and California vote on gay marriage laws in their states in 2009, according to the author?

3. How does Setoodeh define the term "post-gay"?

Even if you've never seen *Glee*, the Fox dramedy with show tunes in its veins and opera in its nervous system, you probably know that it's TV's gayest product since [fitness celebrity] Richard Simmons. Last week's episode [in November 2009] centered on a singing contest of "Defying Gravity," the anticonformity anthem from *Wicked*, every tween girl's favorite musical. The contestants: Rachel the glee-club diva vs. Kurt the, um—what's the male version of diva? Kurt (Chris Colfer) wears fluffy Alexander McQueen sweaters and sings notes high enough to make your fillings hurt. He can belt Beyoncé's "Single Ladies" and thrust his hips better than Ms. Knowles herself. Yet he can also melt your heart with his fortitude and frankness, especially during his fraught talks with his dad, a mechanic who still remembers when his son wore high heels—as a toddler. That's the thing about Kurt: he can be endearing, but he's also confusing. In one episode, the glee club split into a boys' team and a girls' team. Guess which side Kurt went for? If Kurt were transgendered, all that would make perfect sense, but he's not. Instead, he's that oldest of clichés: the sensitive gay boy who really wants to be a girl.

Not that there's anything wrong with that. Really. If the gay community has stood for anything in the 40 years since Stonewall [the 1969 uprising by New York's gay community at the Stonewall Inn that sparked the gay rights movement], it's the freedom not just to love who you want but to be who you are: we're here, we're queer, get used to it. For a while, TV got with the program. In 1997, when [gay actress] Ellen DeGeneres came out on her sitcom, she paved the way for gay characters of every stripe. The next year, *Dawson's Creek* introduced a studly jock named Jack (Kerr Smith), who became perhaps the first teen to come out in prime time. TV's other Jack (Sean Hayes), from *Will & Grace*, swung the more flamboyant way, while lawyerly Will (Eric McCormack) could have been just another "Friend." Over time, the image of gay people on TV became less lavender and more gray—as multifaceted as the five men on *Queer Eye for the Straight Guy* or the ladies of *The L Word*. By bringing all these diverse folks into America's living rooms, TV helped bring gays into the mainstream. A survey by the Gay & Lesbian Alliance Against Defamation found that of the people who say their feelings toward gays and lesbians had become more favorable in the past five years, about one third credited that in part to characters they saw on TV.

In the past year [2009], however, the public-acceptance pendulum seems to have shifted back, at least for what is arguably the biggest test of equality. Two weeks ago, the people of Maine followed the people of California in reversing existing laws that had legalized gay marriage. In fact, when gay marriage has been put before the voters of any state, it has failed every time. Is TV to blame for this? Of course not. The mission of popular culture is to entertain, not to lecture. But if we accept that *Will, Dawson's*, and the rest once fostered acceptance, it's fair to ask if *Glee* may be hurting it, especially because the Kurt model is everywhere. There's Marc (Michael Urie), the flaming fashion assistant on *Ugly Betty*; Lloyd (Rex Lee), Ari's sassy receptionist on *Entourage*; the gay couple on *Modern Family* (one guy still pines for his ice-skating career; the other wears purple in every episode). The fey way extends to nonfiction, too, from the dozens of squealing contestants on *Project Runway* to the two gayest words in the English language: Perez Hilton [celebrity gossip blogger]. Next week *American Idol* runner-up Adam Lambert's new album, *For Your Entertainment*, arrives: that's Lambert on the cover, wearing heavy mascara, black nail polish, and perfect lip gloss. Lesbians face a different problem. They are invariably played by gorgeous, curvy women straight out of a straight man's fantasy—Olivia Wilde on *House*, Sara Ramirez on *Grey's Anatomy*, Evan Rachel Wood on *True Blood*—and they're usually bisexual. How convenient.

Minority groups have long struggled to balance assimilation and extinction, self-expression and alienation. Some African-Americans are complaining that the poor, uneducated girl in *Precious* perpetuates stereotypes; others say she represents a part of the community and deserves to be celebrated. For gays, that schism falls along generational lines. Older gays who spent their lives fighting for civil rights continue to want to stand out, to argue that acceptance means nothing if it doesn't apply to the most outré members. Younger men and women, for whom society has been more tolerant, think of themselves as "post-gay," meaning their sexual orientation is only a part of who they are. Last month [October 2009], gay groups held a march on Washington [DC] for marriage. The older folks gave speeches. The younger ones seemed more interested in snapping a Facebook picture of Lady Gaga.

The problem with the *Glee* club is that Kurt and the rest are loud and proud, but their generation has turned down the volume. All this at a time when standing apart seems particularly counterproductive. Marriage (and the military) are sacred institutions, so it's not surprising that some heterosexuals will defend them against what they see as a radical alteration. But if you want to be invited to someone else's party, sometimes you have to dress the part. Is that a form of appeasement? Maybe. It's not that gay men and women should pretend to be straight, or file down all their fabulously spiky edges. But even Rachel Maddow [lesbian political analyst and host of MSNBC's *The Rachel Maddow Show*] wears lipstick on TV. The key is balance. There's so much more to the gay community than the people on TV (or at a gay-pride parade). We just want a chance to live and love like everybody else. Unfortunately, at the rate we're going, we won't get there until the post-post-gay generation.

> "Between the influence of received ste-
> reotypes and the restrictions of censors,
> gays who did not fit rigid, popularly
> assimilable molds had little place in
> nineties network comedy period."

Gay Roles on Television Have Evolved Beyond Stereotypes

Kevin Hilke

Kevin Hilke is an editor and writer. In the following viewpoint, he explores the evolving stereotypes of gays on television through an examination of the portrayal of gay stereotypes on the 1990s show Seinfeld *and the 2000s show* The Office. *Hilke contends that the gay character of Oscar on* The Office *is one that confounds gay stereotypes and is unique because his sexuality is incidental to his character.*

As you read, consider the following questions:

1. When did "The Outing" air on NBC, according to the author?

2. Who, according to Hilke, was outed in the "The Outing"?

3. How does the character of Oscar defy gay stereotypes in "The Secret", according to the author?

In "The Outing," an iconic 1993 episode of NBC's *Seinfeld* (1989–1998), Jerry Seinfeld (Jerry Seinfeld) and George Costanza (Jason Alexander) are mistakenly outed as homosexuals by Sharon Leonard (Paula Marshall), an NYU [New York University] journalism graduate student who eavesdrops on a conversation among Elaine Benes (Julia Louis-Dreyfus), Jerry, and George at Monk's Café about the most unattractive world leader of all time. The Elaine of *Seinfeld*'s earlier seasons is acid-tongued. She declares that [former Israeli prime minister] Golda Meir could make all other candidates run up a tree. Upon noticing that Sharon, with whom the group is not yet acquainted, is eavesdropping, Elaine puckishly engineers their conversation to imply, for Sharon's benefit, that Jerry and George are gay. Elaine spins her yarn, attempting with George's help to convince Jerry to participate in the ruse, and Jerry resists, comparing his friends to Nazi collaborators: "I'm not going along! I can just see you in Berlin in 1939 goosestepping past me: 'Come on, Jerry, go along, go along!'"

Playing Off Stereotype

This association of homosexuality and Nazism on Jerry's part is incidental, the consequence of a facetious speculative analogy, but the American popcultural Nazi stereotype does nevertheless share a key characteristic of the gay male stereotype as constructed by the *Seinfeld* episode's progression: an anal-retentive valorization of, and unflinching demand for, neatness and order. Aside from Jerry's abnormally-tight turtleneck—almost certainly chosen especially for this scene—among the only plausible bits of evidence for his supposed homosexuality, he tells Elaine and George, is his neatness:

JERRY You know I hear that all the time.

ELAINE Hear what?

JERRY That I'm gay, people think I'm gay.

ELAINE Yeah, you know, people ask me that about you too.

JERRY Yeah because I'm single, I'm thin, and I'm neat.

Neatness here is taken as evidence of gayness. Indeed, it is absolutely essential to the way in which Sharon's article—initially published in an NYU campus paper, then picked up by the *New York Post*—implies Jerry's homosexuality. Sharon is careful never to make an explicit claim about Jerry's sexuality, instead recounting an anecdote that superficially maintains his straightness while strongly suggesting that he and George are a gay couple: "Within the confines of his fastidious bachelor pad," she writes, "Seinfeld and Costanza bicker over the cleanliness of a piece of fruit like an old married couple." Sharon's case, as she presents it, rests largely on Jerry and George's ostensible obsession with cleanliness. Jerry's stand-up routine concluding "The Outing" cements neatness as a central characteristic of homosexuality, even going so far as to suggest that making a vacuuming noise—a symbol of cleanliness—should become conversational shorthand for implying that a man is gay:

> I am not gay. I am, however, thin, single and neat. Sometimes when someone is thin, single and neat people assume they are gay because that is a stereotype. [...] If people are even going to assume that people that are neat are gay, maybe instead of doin' this: "Y'know I think Joe might be a little ... [*waves hand back and forth*]", they should vacuum: "Y'know I think Joe might be *VROOM*; [*makes vacuuming motion*]. Yeah, I got a feeling he's a little *VROOM*...."

Jerry does challenge this cleanliness stereotype, expressing sympathy for gays who might face discrimination for their sloppiness. Despite this, the vision of homosexuality the episode ultimately offers is anchored in an almost military proclivity for cleanliness. Jerry may want to solace dirty homos,

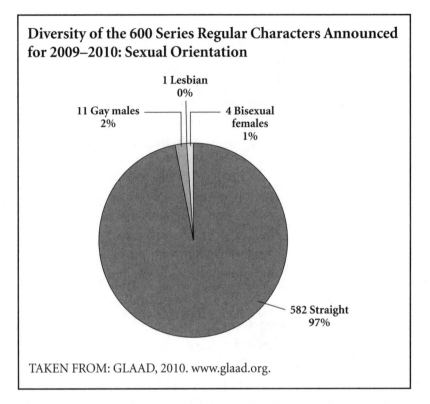

Diversity of the 600 Series Regular Characters Announced for 2009–2010: Sexual Orientation

1 Lesbian
0%

11 Gay males
2%

4 Bisexual females
1%

582 Straight
97%

TAKEN FROM: GLAAD, 2010. www.glaad.org.

but they have no place in this episode other than as objects of pity, as sites of at least three potential traumas: that of homosexuality as such, that of rejection by stereotypical homosexuals, and that of estrangement from mainstream society for failing to fit the received, digestible, user-friendly cultural stereotype.

NBC Evolves the Stereotype

Between the influence of received stereotypes and the restrictions of censors, gays who did not fit rigid, popularly assimilable molds had little place in nineties network comedy period. NBC's programming, especially, suffered from this sort of stereotyping, culminating in the unabashedly stereotype-perpetuating, and thus user-friendly, *Will & Grace* (which is nonetheless innovative in its own right). Now, fifteen years after Jerry's outing, NBC's offers us *The Office*'s Oscar Martinez

(Oscar Nuñez), a gay member of Dunder-Mifflin Scranton's three-person accounting department whose character debuts as ostensibly straight. Oscar is revolutionary in network TV comedy not because he defies outmoded stereotypes, which he does, but because his homosexuality—along with what his culturally insensitive boss, Michael Scott (Steve Carell), terms his "Mexicanity"—is kept consistently incidental to his character.

The first time we meaningfully meet Oscar, in the second episode of the first season, "Diversity Day," not only is he *not* introduced as a homosexual—downplaying, in retrospect, the importance of homosexuality to the constitution of his character beyond his choice of sexual partner—he *is* introduced as an examplar of another stereotype: Mexicanity. But Oscar no more embodies Mexican or Chicano or Hispanic stereotypes than he embodies gay stereotypes; he is nothing but a symbol: Oscar, for Michael, *stands for* Mexican, just as customer service representative Kelly Kapoor stands for Indian and salesman Stanley Hudson stands for black. Beyond these nominal symbolic roles, Oscar has no particular relationship, for us, to either homosexuality or Mexicanity.

What Is "The Secret"?

When we do find out that Oscar is gay, it is by accident. Oscar is outed for the audience—in the second season episode "The Secret"—as a fortuitous result of an investigation by Dwight Schrute (Rainn Wilson), Michael's number-two, into whether the sick day Oscar has taken is legitimate. The title of the episode might at first seem to highlight Oscar's "secret," and to an extent it does. In Oscar's mind. Dwight, upon finding Oscar arriving at his home with his partner Gil, has discovered that Oscar is gay. Dwight, who tells Oscar simply that he won't "tell Michael," doesn't realize Oscar is gay. The secret he believes himself to be keeping for Oscar—in return for a favor redeemable at a time and place of his choosing—is that Oscar has taken an illegitimate sick day. The episode's primary storyline concerns the revelation of yet another secret, a third vying for representation by the title, and the one having the greatest effect on the volition of the show: that salesman Jim Halpert (John Krasinski) had and perhaps still has feelings for receptionist Pam Beesley (Jenna Fischer). The secret of Oscar's homosexuality is certainly referred to by the title, but it is by no means the title's sole referent. It comes to us as an incidental consequence of an investigation that produces a second, more widely-revealed secret—Oscar's attendance "malfeasance," in Dwight's term. Both of these secrets concerning Oscar are then largely eclipsed by a third, stage-stealing secret concerning Jim and Pam: the starting point for what would become the program's primary storyline over the next three seasons. Although the secret of Oscar's homosexuality is submerged beneath these other secrets for Oscar's fellow characters, it is for us perhaps the most potent secret of the three: we alone share it with him. Yet knowledge of his homosexuality changes nothing about his character. Oscar's homosexuality is both undeniable and unspeakable; but it is neither flamboyant nor timid. It is simply there.

Wonderfully, and in a confounding of *Seinfeld*-era stereotypes, it is Oscar's defiance of cleanliness—which is both stereotypically gay and, for Michael, stereotypically Mexican—that leads us to discover that he's gay. Dwight launches his investigation in "The Secret" not simply because Oscar has taken a day off, but because in doing so, Oscar has refused to participate in the office's "spring cleaning" day. When Michael calls Oscar's home to confirm that he is indeed there recuperating, he casts Oscar's refusal in terms of his Mexicanity: "You know it's cleaning day here today? Coulda' used some of that famous Hispanic cleaning ethic!" Oscar won't be cleaning that day, but it has nothing to do with his ethnicity or his sexuality. He just wants a day off.

| "It's no wonder high-ranking lawyers in the [George W.] Bush administration erected an entire torture policy around the fictional edifice of Jack Bauer."

Television Promotes Torture

Dahlia Lithwick

Dahlia Lithwick is a columnist for Slate, *an online periodical. In the following viewpoint, she contends that the guiding character behind the US torture policy during the George W. Bush administration was Jack Bauer from the television show* 24. *Lithwick juxtaposes the fictional premises of* 24 *against the real-life situation and consequences of authorizing torture, underscoring the absurdity of building a torture policy around a fictional character.*

As you read, consider the following questions:

1. According to the author, what did British lawyer and writer Philippe Sands say about Jack Bauer's role in discussions of military officials in 2002?

2. How did former Department of Homeland Security chief Michael Chertoff describe 24, according to Lithwick?

3. How did Supreme Court justice Antonin Scalia feel
about convicting Jack Bauer, according to the author?

The most influential legal thinker in the development of
modern American interrogation policy is not a behavioral
psychologist, international lawyer, or counterinsurgency expert. Reading both Jane Mayer's stunning *The Dark Side* and
Philippe Sands' *The Torture Team*, I quickly realized that the
prime mover of American interrogation doctrine is none other
than the star of Fox Television's *24*: Jack Bauer.

This fictional counterterrorism agent—a man never at a
loss for something to do with an electrode—has his finger-
prints all over U.S. interrogation policy. As Sands and Mayer
tell it, the lawyers designing interrogation techniques cited
Bauer more frequently than the Constitution.

24 as Inspiration

According to British lawyer and writer Philippe Sands, Jack
Bauer—played by Kiefer Sutherland—was an inspiration at
early "brainstorming meetings" of military officials at Guan-
tanamo [Bay detention center in Cuba] in September of 2002.
Diane Beaver, the staff judge advocate general who gave legal
approval to 18 controversial new interrogation techniques including water-boarding, sexual humiliation, and terrorizing
prisoners with dogs, told Sands that Bauer "gave people lots of
ideas." Michael Chertoff, the homeland-security chief, once
gushed in a panel discussion on *24* organized by the Heritage
Foundation that the show "reflects real life."

John Yoo, the former Justice Department lawyer who produced the so-called torture memos—simultaneously redefin-
ing both the laws of torture and logic—cites Bauer in his
book *War by Other Means*. "What if, as the popular Fox television program *24* recently portrayed, a high-level terrorist
leader is caught who knows the location of a nuclear weapon?"
Even Supreme Court Justice Antonin Scalia, speaking in

Torture on Television

In both 1996 and 1997, there were no prime-time TV scenes containing torture, according to the Parents Television Council [PTC], which keeps a programming database. In 2003, there were 228 such scenes, the PTC said. The count was over 100 in both 2004 and 2005.

David Bauder, USA Today, *February 11, 2007.*

Canada last summer [in 2007], shows a gift for this casual toggling between television and the Constitution. "Jack Bauer saved Los Angeles. . . . He saved hundreds of thousands of lives," Scalia said. "Are you going to convict Jack Bauer?"

Ticking Time Bombs All Over the Place

There are many reasons that matriculation from the Jack Bauer School of Law would have encouraged even the most cautious legal thinkers to bend and eventually break the longstanding rules against torture. U.S. interrogators rarely if ever encounter a "ticking time bomb," someone with detailed information about an imminent terror plot. But according to the Parents' Television Council (one of several advocacy groups to have declared war on *24*), Jack Bauer encounters a "ticking time-bomb" an average of 12 times per season. Given that each season allegedly represents a 24-hour period, Bauer encounters someone who needs torturing 12 times each day! Experienced interrogators know that information extracted through torture is rarely reliable. But Jack Bauer's torture not only elicits the truth, it does so before commercial. He is a human polygraph who has a way with flesh-eating chemicals.

It's no wonder high-ranking lawyers in the [George W.] Bush administration erected an entire torture policy around the fictional edifice of Jack Bauer. He's a hero. Men want to be him, and women want to be there to hand him the electrical cord. John Yoo wanted to change American torture law to accommodate him, and Justice Scalia wants to immunize him from prosecution. The problem is not just that they all saw themselves in Jack Bauer. The problem was their failure to see what Jack Bauer really represents in relation to the legal universe of *24*.

The Truth About Jack Bauer

For one thing, Jack Bauer operates outside the law, and he knows it. Nobody in the fictional world of *24* changes the rules to permit him to torture. For the most part, he does so fully aware that he is breaking the law. Bush administration officials turned that formula on its head. In an almost Nixonian [like President Richard Nixon] twist, the new interrogation doctrine seems to have become: "If Jack Bauer does it, it can't be illegal."

Bauer is also willing to accept the consequences of his decisions to break the law. In fact, that is the real source of his heroism—to the extent one finds torture heroic. He makes a moral choice at odds with the prevailing system and accepts the consequences of the system's judgment by periodically reinventing a whole new identity for himself or enduring punishment at the hands of foreign governments. The "heroism" of the Bush administration's torture apologists is slightly less inspiring. None of them is willing to stand up and admit, as Bauer does, that yes, they did "whatever it takes." They instead point fingers and cry, "Witch hunt."

Real-Life Consequences

If you're a fan of *24*, you'll enjoy *The Dark Side*. There you will meet Mamdouh Habib, an Australian captured in Pakistan, beaten by American interrogators with what he believed to be an "electric cattle prod," and threatened with rape by dogs. He confessed to all sorts of things that weren't true. He was released after three years without charges. You'll also meet Maher Arar, a Canadian engineer who experienced pretty much the same story, save that the beatings were with electrical cables. Arar was also released without explanation. He's been cleared of any links to terrorism by the Canadian government. Jack Bauer would have known these men were not "ticking time bombs" inside of 10 minutes. Our real-life heroes had to torture them for years before realizing they were innocent.

That is, of course, the punch line. The lawyers who were dead set on unleashing an army of Jack Bauers against our enemies built a whole torture policy around a fictional character. But Bauer himself could have told them that one Jack Bauer—a man who deliberately lives outside the boundaries of law—would have been more than enough.

"The torture scenes, as much as they endorse the ticking-clock argument, still leave a bad aftertaste."

Television Reflects National Debate on Torture

Chris Barsanti

Chris Barsanti is a writer and a member of the New York Film Critics Online. In the following viewpoint, he argues that the television show 24 has a lot of fans because it reflects the anxieties of living in our current era. Barsanti argues that the show presents a complicated picture of the moral debate around the issue of torture, which reflects the American national debate.

As you read, consider the following questions:

1. According to Anne Applebaum, quoted by the author, how does the torture debate break down?

2. Why do conservative publications like the *National Review* and *Washington Times* praise *24*, according to Barsanti?

3. How does the author believe that *24* "hedges like a good liberal"?

When the debate was raging over the airwaves and in the Washington halls of power over whether or not [vice president Dick] Cheney and his shadow government pals should be allowed to circumvent torture prohibitions, the argument often seemed not so much "Is torture right?" but "Does torture work?" It's a kind of grim calculus that skirts morality and asks instead how much immorality must one accept and pragmatically embrace in the world. As [*Washington Post*] columnist Anne Applebaum pointed out in "The Torture Myth", the debate breaks down along pretty predictable party lines, with humanitarian liberals assuming that torture never works (ignoring any evidence to the contrary), and "realists," whether liberal or conservative, who tended to eagerly accept fake accounts of effective torture. Testosterone-soaked pundits played the realist card while prominent veteran [Senator] John McCain kindly pointed out that when he was [a prisoner of war] tortured by the North Vietnamese wanting the names of other men in his unit, he gave them the names of the Green Bay Packers [football team] starting line, just to stop the pain. According to some media critics, there's another constituency that believes full well that torture works, namely the viewers of *24*.

Torture on *24*

Fox's series—which loads 24 hours of real-time apocalypse scenarios into each season—just kicked off its fifth season (or "day") with a tension-junkie four-hour, two-night spread of the worst their writers could come up with to throw at jaded viewers. A former president is assassinated, terrorists take hostages at an airport and hey, where did all that nerve gas come from? This is all in a typical season for a show that dishes out the terror like sitcoms do canned laughter. On *24*, favorite characters get killed off, the country's leadership seems weak and disorganized, and the apocalypse is nigh. One of the only standards that their writers didn't include in the first four hours (though they got to it soon after) was a torture scene, which previously had been showing up with dreary regularity in a show which has more than once—and not without reason—been referred to as "torture porn".

The reason for this is simple. Fairly often during the show, an agent of CTU (the show's fictitious Counter Terrorism Unit, which has shockingly poor employee screening techniques but otherwise acts like the efficient and elite evil-fighting force we all wish existed but deep down know doesn't) attempts to pry information from a recalcitrant suspect. The CTU agent (usually Jack Bauer, the show's grim-visaged star played by Kiefer Sutherland) then resorts to violently gruesome methods which often yield the required information.

This wouldn't be so troubling—nastier things happen in film and TV all the time—were it not for the fact that the show counts among its fan base plenty of rabid conservatives (including, rumor has it, many White House staffers [in the George W. Bush administration]) whom one can easily imagine on the couch, cheering Jack on as he acts out all their darker impulses which the Democrat wimps want to curtail. Right-wing bulldogs like *The National Review* and *The Washington Times* praise the show for its "realism" and (what they see as) its refusal to play the game of Hollywood liberals. The show's complement of consultants is peppered with ex-government Intel types and [military espionage novelist] Tom Clancy-esque writers like Vince Flynn who are adept at coming up with scenarios in which the bad guys (Russian separatists this season, Muslim fundamentalists in the last one) push the limits of what can be combated with humane methods.

Ethical Gray Areas

A classic example of these ethically gray areas came up in a recent episode. Agent Bauer is trying to get information out of a highly-placed White House mole who refuses to talk—that is, until Bauer holds a knife to his eye and says, "You've read my file" as a way of intimating what he'll do. Surprise, surprise, the mole antes up. This is the classic "ticking-clock" scenario that the pro-torture realists always speak of in which the ethical compromise of torture is weighed against the need to gain information immediately to prevent imminent harm against others. [Lawyer and political commentator] Alan Dershowitz raised holy hell a couple years ago when he made the case for torture under these circumstances, even going so far as to suggest getting a judge's approval for it, through the issuance of a "torture warrant".

What nobody on either side of this debate has managed to conclusively state is whether or not such ticking-clock scenarios actually happen (likely the people who do know for sure are bound by secrecy laws not to say anything). Being fiction—an important distinction that many of its critics miss—*24* can neatly bypass this uncertainty by the mere fact of its real-time structure: *the clock is always ticking*. In the real world, even the Israeli government—who have more need of time-sensitive information than any other government in the world, not to mention more experience with interrogating terror suspects—has sworn off the use of interrogation by torture as it hasn't been proven to yield reliable Intel (refer again to McCain's Green Bay Packers gambit). It just doesn't work.

24 Justifies Torture

Does *24* justify torture? Absolutely. The show excuses its characters going beyond the law when necessary in the time-honored tradition of *Dirty Harry*, in which [actor] Clint Eastwood dispensed with legal niceties. So much so that famed *New Yorker* critic, Pauline Kael labeled the film "fascist". Just as Dirty Harry Callahan exemplified the right-wing push-back against namby-pamby civil rights in the early years of rulings like *Miranda v. Arizona* (1966) that curtailed law enforcers' ability to act with impunity, *24* puts itself pretty squarely on the "pro" side of the torture debate.

One of the show's more ridiculous scenes came last season [2005] when an accomplice of that season's villain, Marwan, gets brought into CTU for questioning (i.e., torture). Marwan gets on the phone to an ACLU [American Civil Liberties Union]/Amnesty International-esque group called Amnesty Global, and within minutes (this is after midnight in LA, mind you), one of their lawyers shows up and gets the prisoner sprung. Never mind the fact that human rights lawyers have about as much power to do such things as you or I, the primary problem here is that the show gets its clichés wrong. In your standard law-and-order narrative, the sleazy, sports-car-driving, thousand-dollar-suit-wearing attorney is supposed to be a criminal defense lawyer, the kind who gets rich off keeping drug dealers out of jail by any Machiavellian means necessary. In what world do *24*'s writers live in which human rights lawyers drive sports cars and dress like Hugo Boss models instead of puttering around in sticker-covered Volvos and wearing off-the-rack suits from JC Penney? They should at least try to get their clichés right.

Show Has a Liberal Side, Too

That said, *24* also hedges like a good liberal. Because even though Bauer has a predilection for torture—you wince anytime a suspect is brought in, just waiting for the implements to be brought out—viewers' more Neanderthal tendencies are rarely if ever rewarded with a clean conclusion. The show never provides the kind of expected action-film climax where the chisel-faced hero, having looked into the void of evil and partaken of its dark tools, finally offs the villain to applause from the balcony. For every liberal-baiting scene like the one described just above, there's several in which CTU and the forces of law and order get it wrong. At least three times last season, either the wrong person was tortured or was tortured and didn't provide any information. And in the early episodes of the new season, a persnickety CTU official (played by Sean

The Appeal of Torture Television

Howard Gordon, an executive producer of *24*, suggested that a helpless feeling in the nation because of terrorism and the Iraq war may be what creators are reflecting in their shows. There's been a surge in general in the level of violence tolerated in prime time.

"Perhaps at some level it's an expression of our anger and our helplessness," he said.

David Bauder,
USA Today, *February 11, 2007.*

Astin) who looked at first like the kind of spineless desk jockey so often lampooned in testosterone fiction turns out to be better at his job than just about any of the show regulars due to his by-the-book bureaucratic ways.

In a somewhat garbled essay published recently in *The Guardian* (12 January 2006) called "The Depraved Heroes of *24* are the Himmlers of Hollywood", Lacanian [referring to French psychoanalyst Jacques Lacan] psychoanalytic pop culture fulminator Slavoj Zizek compared the show's "depraved" protagonists to Nazis. Zizek's basic point is that by portraying the CTU agents as still somehow noble and heroic after performing such inhuman deeds, the show caters to the same deluded lie that Nazi operatives like [Adolf] Eichmann and [Heinrich] Himmler believed, "that it is not only possible to retain human dignity in performing acts of terror, but that if an honest person performs such an act as a grave duty, it confers on him a tragical-ethical grandeur." Though full of 180-proof ivory-tower exaggeration, there's some truth in Zizek's comparison here, but it lacks a solid knowledge of the show itself, especially the way it handles its characters.

There Are Repercussions

To completely buy Zizek's argument, one would have to claim that *24* lets its characters who partake in such acts off the hook, which is hardly the case. Just as, at the end of *Dirty Harry*, Clint throws his badge away, by the show's fifth season, Bauer has utterly ruined himself for his country, losing his family, friends and practically any semblance of humanity. It would be one thing if everything ended happily, with a pained Bauer stalking off into the tragically grand sunset and everyone else celebrating. The torture scenes, as much as they endorse the ticking-clock argument, still leave a bad aftertaste.

All of this could simply be my attempt to rationalize my love of a show whose politics and morals I have good reason to suspect are quite at odds with my own. That is, I *want* to see that Bauer and his compatriots don't really want to do the things they have to do, and are spiritually wrecked by it afterward, as a means of justifying how thrilling I find the show, which is like an action soap opera for the post-9/11 era. A friend who's a near-fanatic *24* devotee and self-identified "old-school liberal," puts it more clearly: "Do I think *24* romanticizes torture? Heck yeah I do. But it's a TV show. Its function is to stir me. Scare me. Act out what my imagination's darkest corners wouldn't even consider."

The darkest corner of *my* imagination is a place where one could commit these horrible acts against another person and yet have nothing to show for it in the end, even after one has gone down that dead-end road. Although I know its patently absurd ticking-clock situations make a mockery of the real debate on torture, in its constant doom-seeking *24* seems a show less about torture than about nightmares, where the most hopeless situation usually gets worse, regardless of how many rules are broken to make it right. If Bauer's spiritually exhausted, dead-eyed visage means anything to me, it is an advertisement for what torture does, not just to those it is inflicted on, but also to those who perform it. Nobody gets away clean.

Periodical Bibliography

The following articles have been selected to supplement the diverse views presented in this chapter.

P. Ryan Baber   "Trans America," *Hollywood Reporter*, April 25, 2008.

David Bauder   "Group: TV Torture Influencing Real Life," *USA Today*, February 11, 2007.

Katy Elliot   "A Crisis in Values?" *Broadcast*, March 14, 2008.

James Emery   "Arab Culture and Muslim Stereotypes," *World and I*, May 2008.

Dale Hrabi   "The Lambert Factor," *The Advocate*, June–July 2009.

Irene Lacher   "Out of the Box," *Hollywood Reporter*, April 13, 2007.

Patrick McCormick   "The Torture Show," *U.S. Catholic*, May 2008.

Newsweek   "Snide and Prejudice," October 15, 2007.

Virginia Postrel   "Beautiful Minds," *Atlantic*, September 2007.

Kathyrn Reklis   "Prime-Time Torture: Jack Bauer as a Hero of Our Time," *Christian Century*, June 2008.

Choire Sicha   "Relax—It's Just TV," *Advocate*, July 1, 2008.

Monica Trasandes   "Are We Visible Yet?" *Advocate*, February 1, 2005.

Variety   "Stereotypes: Reality TV's Dirty Little Secret," January 11, 2010.

OPPOSING
VIEWPOINTS®
SERIES

CHAPTER 2

What Are the Issues of Reality Television?

Chapter Preface

Reality television is a genre of television programming that films ordinary people in unscripted situations. In America, reality television has a long history, dating back to the early days of television. Considered the first reality television show, Alan Funt's 1948 series *Candid Camera* used a hidden camera to show how ordinary people dealt with odd surprises and pranks. In 1973, the PBS network aired a groundbreaking documentary-style program, *The Louds*, which filmed the daily lives of a normal American family, the Louds. During the twelve-hour run of the show, which chronicled seven months in the lives of the family, the parents, Bill and Pat Loud, decided to divorce. Lance Loud, the elder son, came out as gay to his family. The show exposed the changing values of the American family and touched on issues that many American families had to deal with in their own lives. Many viewers were shocked by the controversial issues dealt with on the show. Viewers flocked to the real-life drama of *The Louds*, which drew more than ten million viewers for its broadcast and became a pop culture landmark.

In the 1970s reality television become more viable with the introduction of the videocassette format and new portable cameras, which made portable video more affordable and accessible for filmmakers and television stations. People could now go out on the streets with high-quality, transportable cameras to capture real-life situations in quick time. Programs in the 1980s such as *Real People* and *That's Incredible* did just that—and attracted millions of viewers in the process.

However, the advent of what we now recognize as reality television can be traced back to the 1992 premiere of *The Real World* on MTV. This seminal show took seven young adults from different backgrounds and put them in a house to live together for several months, filming their unscripted interactions. Producers gave them a set-up situation, such as a job, a shared vacation, planned outings, but let the individuals react genuinely to each other.

The popularity of reality television in the United States exploded with the introduction of *Survivor* in 2000. *Survivor* is a reality television game show in which a group of ordinary people are cast and then taken to an isolated area in the jungle, wilderness, or desert, to compete for a million-dollar prize. Contestants are split into tribes and form alliances with other contestants to advance, as others are eliminated until a winner becomes the "sole survivor." The show proved immensely popular with the viewing public. It was a staple on the list of top ten television series of the year in its first ten years and is considered the mother of American reality television because of its widespread popularity.

Nowadays reality television is ubiquitous on network and cable television. Consistently popular and cheap to produce, networks are turning to reality television more and more often to fill their programming schedules. The following chapter examines the topical value and exploitative nature of the reality television genre. The viewpoints also debate the educational value of both courtroom and prison television.

| "Reality TV's celebration of egoism and exhibitionism contributes to the fame-at-any-cost mentality that afflicts many teenagers today."

Reality Television Is Exploitative

Colleen Carroll Campbell

Colleen Carroll Campbell is an author, television and radio host, and fellow at the Ethics and Public Policy Center. In the following viewpoint, she argues that the current American media culture—which values fame above all else and celebrates exhibitionists at the expense of true artists—is harmful to American children. Campbell opines that the more time Americans spend watching reality television, the more they will mimic the shows' egotistical and materialistic behaviors.

As you read, consider the following questions:

1. What do Drew Pinsky and S. Mark Young argue in their new book, *The Mirror Effect,* according to Campbell?

Colleen Carroll Campbell, "Exploitative Reality Shows Degrade Us, Too," *St. Louis Post-Dispatch*, June 25, 2009. Reprinted with permission of the St. Louis Post-Dispatch, copyright © 2009.

2. According to a 2006 study in the *Journal of Research in Personality*, as cited by the author, where do television celebrities rank in narcissistic traits?

3. According to a 2005 *Washington Post* survey cited by Campbell, what percentage of American teenagers believe that they will be famous someday?

The excruciatingly public marital troubles between Jon and Kate Gosselin reached their predictable denouement Monday [June 22, 2009], when the reality television stars announced their impeding divorce before an audience of 10.6 million. After 10 years of marriage and two years of filming *Jon & Kate Plus 8*, the parents of 8-year-old twins and 5-year-old sextuplets denied that the constant intrusion of cameras into their private life had precipitated their split or exploited their children. And true to form, the couple assured viewers that the divorce would not interfere with their hit cable series. As Kate Gosselin said gravely, "The show must go on."

That stomach-churning spectacle may prove the last hurrah of this unseemly series, which increasingly has relied on tabloid coverage of the couple's marital woes to boost ratings. If a ratings freefall does not kill the show, legal troubles might: Pennsylvania authorities recently began investigating a complaint about child labor law violations involving the eight Gosselin children, who spend long hours under the glare of the spotlight to satisfy their parents' hankering for money and fame.

Not Harmless Entertainment

It's easy to mock the Gosselin parents and fret over their children, who never asked to have the most painful moments of their childhood broadcast for the world's amusement. But those children are not the only victims of shows like this one.

Our children, too, are endangered by a media culture that promotes voyeurism as entertainment and exalts exhibitionists as role models.

In their new book, *The Mirror Effect*, addiction medicine specialist Drew Pinsky and business professor S. Mark Young argue that following the foibles of reality TV stars and other celebrities is not a wholly harmless pastime. The more time we spend observing the shocking, materialistic and egotistical behavior of reality TV stars, they argue, the more likely we are to mimic that behavior in our own lives and view the pathological self-centeredness of these "Joe Six-Pack" celebrities as normal.

That's troubling, since most reality TV stars are anything but normal. In a 2006 study published in the *Journal of Research in Personality*, Pinsky and Young used the Narcissistic Personality Inventory to assess celebrity egoism. They found that reality TV celebrities ranked highest in narcissistic traits, surpassing even rock stars and actors.

Fame Is Dangerous

Reality TV's celebration of egoism and exhibitionism contributes to the fame-at-any-cost mentality that afflicts many teenagers today. According to a 2005 survey by *The Washington Post*, Henry J. Kaiser Family Foundation and Harvard University, nearly one-third of American teenagers believe they will be famous someday. In Britain, a 2006 Learning and Skills Council study found that more than one in 10 teenagers would forgo an education or training for the chance to appear on TV, and nearly one in 10 consider fame a "great way to earn money without skills or qualifications."

Even among younger children, that lust for fame has fueled some disturbing trends, from "sexting"—the practice of sharing naked pictures of oneself or others via cell phone—to the online posting of "fight videos" by bullies who videotape themselves in the act of brutalizing their peers.

Strategies to Curb a Lust for Fame

How can we curb such destructive fame-chasing? Celebrating a child's legitimate achievements rather than his attention-getting antics is one strategy. Enforcing child labor laws against camera-crazed parents like the Gosselins is another.

When it comes to mitigating the effects of exploitative entertainment like *Jon & Kate Plus 8*, the simplest solution may be the one proposed by Kate Gosselin's brother, Kevin Kreider, who recently made a public appeal on behalf of his nieces and nephews. Urging Americans to remember that the Gosselin children are "not fictional characters," he acknowledged that "Jon and Kate obviously will not quit [the show] on their own."

"So please," Kreider said, "stop watching."

| "The majority of college students watch reality TV to escape from the daily responsibilities of running around campus and studying."

Reality Television Is Escapist Entertainment

Emili Johnson

Emili Johnson is a columnist for the Simpsonian, *a student publication of Simpson College, in Indianola, Iowa. In the following viewpoint, she analyzes the appeal of reality television, asserting that it provides a few minutes of escapist entertainment in an otherwise busy and stressful life.*

As you read, consider the following questions:

1. According to Professor Brian Steffen, as cited by Johnson, how realistic is reality television?

2. Why does college student Alfredo Sanchez watch reality shows, according to the author?

3. Why does Johnson believe that the popularity of reality shows will endure?

Escapist Entertainment

Today's comic escapism seems especially linked to the notion of failure as success—the aim isn't to celebrate the victory so much as to soften the backslide. Watching the real and figurative pratfalls on *Wipeout* and other reality shows feels more satisfying than watching rich people suffer in the standard class-warfare soaps [soap operas]. Even when we look at the privileged these days, we're willing to be generous, as long as their suffering has a comic element. As payback for the continued entertainment she provides, we let [celebrity heiress and reality television actress] Paris Hilton remain in the spotlight indefinitely.

Joanna Weiss,
Boston Globe, July 27, 2008.

No matter what anyone says, everyone knows that they have at least one favorite reality TV show. It doesn't matter if it's NBC's *The Apprentice*, The CW Network's *America's Next Top Model* or ABC's *The Bachelor*. There is at least one show that will distract you from doing your homework and keep you entertained for at least an hour.

The idea of reality TV, which was at one point in time meant to show real people doing real things and fulfilling real goals, has now been turned into an easier way for ordinary people to become famous. The contestants may be duped by a lying "millionaire," in search of their soul mate or may be getting even with the mean girls at school. These contestants are far from being real people with real problems doing real things. They are looking for their fifteen minutes of fame and as long as the camera is rolling we will be watching.

The Appeal of Reality Television

As college students, we spend a great deal of time in class, at club meetings and at The Zoo [a local bar]. When we are in front of the TV, the majority of the time we are watching some reality TV show to see who will be the next person to go home or who is crying because their dream did not come true.

This made me think about why we watch so much reality TV to begin with. My favorite reality TV shows at the moment are *I Love New York* on VH1 and *America's Next Top Model* on the CW Network. During the time that I am watching these two shows, homework goes unfinished and phone calls are missed. I need to know how the drama unfolds on my shows.

So, the general question is, why do we watch so much reality TV if we have our own lives to live? What makes the people in the shows attractive to a wide audience? Do these images really represent reality?

Reality Television Is Not Realistic

Pondering these questions, I went to Brian Steffen, professor of communication studies. While he does not have any favorite reality shows, he did mention that the majority of reality TV is in fact unrealistic.

"Reality TV is, in fact, probably the least real thing on TV," Steffen said. "I think a cartoon like *The Simpsons* is ten times more realistic than any reality program such as *Laguna Beach*."

Steffen also mentioned that our society is wrapped in the idea that being a well-known celebrity is an instant ticket into the glamorous life. It will save us from being ordinary, which is one of the worst sins you can commit in American culture.

Escapist Entertainment

The majority of students who watch reality TV do it for entertainment and as a break from studying to see the drama unfold on a wide variety of shows.

Junior Alfredo Sanchez has been watching reality shows such as *The Real World* and *Survivor* for about as long as both shows have been on TV. He feels that while producers of *The Real World* do tend to cast wild and crazy people with monumental problems, it is still something to watch and be entertained by.

"Most of the time, I watch reality shows because I am bored and there's nothing better on (TV) and it keeps me entertained." Sanchez said.

The majority of college students watch reality TV to escape from the daily responsibilities of running around campus and studying. It is nice to come back to your room from a long day of classes, meetings and practices and be able to see the drama among *The Real World* housemates or see teams duke it out for money on *Survivor*.

A Break from Real Life

Yes, it is unrealistic to have the chance to choose your soul mate out of a group of twenty contestants, but that's what makes it entertaining. We know that it may not happen to us, but it is always interesting to see what decisions someone else will make and it is even more intriguing to see someone make a complete fool of themselves for the sake of one's heart. In today's world, that's what makes great television.

We may never see the end of reality TV because now that people know how easy it is to get their fifteen minutes of fame, everyone will always be trying to reach that goal of true celebrity. Fortunately for the rest of us, there will always be a camera rolling to document every minute of it.

> "As an unapologetic producer of reality shows, . . . [I] know that any genre that provokes such howls of protest is doing something interesting."

Reality Television Addresses Hot-Button Issues

Michael Hirschorn

Michael Hirschorn is a contributing editor for the Atlantic. *In the following viewpoint, he argues that reality shows expose a community's shared value system and "render emotional truths." Hirschorn asserts that reality television has also inspired documentary filmmakers such as Michael Moore to push the envelope in their own work.*

As you read, consider the following questions:

1. How does the author feel that the show *Wife Swap* deals with value systems?

2. According to Hirschorn, how has reality television inspired documentary filmmaking?

3. According to the author, what does Michael Moore do with children who were shot at Columbine High School in his movie *Bowling for Columbine*?

In *Real Housewives*, businessman Lou Knickerbocker stages a photo shoot to promote his new "highly oxygenated" water, variously called "Aqua Air" and "O.C. Energy Drink" ("We have patented technology that produces water from air"). The models are attractive-ish teen and 20-something girls: Lou's daughter Lindsey, by ex-wife Tammy; a few other daughters of O.C. [Orange County, California,] housewives; and a newcomer whom Lou apparently found waitressing at a local restaurant.

Lou and Tammy made piles of money—it's not clear how—but their finances seem to have fractured along with their marriage. The photo shoot, therefore, is throwing off more than the normal amount of flop sweat. Lou apparently has personally selected the girls, which means he has declined to showcase his other daughter, Megan, because of her tattoos and lack of physical fitness. Lou believes the "Aqua Air Angels" should embody the Aqua Air ideal, which is why they can't drink or smoke and must have grade-point averages higher than 3.5. "This is a photo shoot," he barks after a fight breaks out between one of the girls and the waitress, "not a gang bang, for chrissakes."

Reflection of a Community's Value System

The detail is what puts the scene over: Lou's lip-smacking focus on the girls, the girls' bland acquiescence. "That's it, baby, smile," Lou urges his daughter. "Show those teeth," says Tammy. A similar scenario on *Desperate Housewives* could never have been quite this preposterous, quite this blandly amoral. The characters would have been scripted with softening, redeeming qualities, or been rendered comically evil. Lou would've gotten his comeuppance, like Wallace Shawn's

Reality in Reality Television

The best reality shows can be much more engrossing, complex and diverse than your average TV cop show. Last year [in 2009] *The Amazing Race* included the team of bisexual screenwriter Mike White and his gay minister father Mel White, giving a more nuanced, less stereotypical portrayal of both sexual orientation and faith than most big-network dramas would.

The past decade has seen experiments like documentary maker Morgan Spurlock's *30 Days* for FX, a brilliant trading-places switcheroo. . . . *Wife Swap* is an intriguing show about American subcultures (homeschoolers, political activists, etc.) and the natural tendency of parents to secretly judge one another. TLC's *19 Kids and Counting*, about the fecund Duggars, may be an extreme-parenting freak show, but it's also a series about the life of a deeply religious family, a rare subject for TV dramas today.

Even MTV, home of *Jersey Shore*, has . . . *My Life as Liz*, a sort of reality *My So-Called Life* about a high school outcast in small-town Texas.

James Poniewozik,
Time, February 22, 2010.

money-siphoning literary agent in that series. Here, the apparent willingness of the young women and at least some of the parents to indulge Lou's bottom-of-the-barrel scheming outlines, in a few short brushstrokes, a community's shared value system.

Value systems are smashed into each other, like atoms in an accelerator, on ABC's *Wife Swap*, where the producers find the most extreme pairings possible: lesbian mommies with bigots, godless cosmopolites with Bible thumpers. On one

February [2007] show, a Pentacostal family, the Hoovers, was paired with the family of a former pastor, Tony Meeks, who has turned from God to follow his rock-and-roll dreams (mom Tish rocks out as well). "I feel by being there," Kristin Hoover said, "I was able to remind Tony that God still loves him and is not finished with him." The episode took seriously the Hoovers' commitment to homeschooling and their rejection of contemporary culture (a rejection not taken to the extreme of declining an invitation to appear on reality TV). Compare this with the tokenism of "born-again Christian" Harriet Hayes on NBC's dramedy *Studio 60 on the Sunset Strip*. Harriet's but a cipher, a rhetorical backboard against which ex-boyfriend Matt Albie can thwack his heathen wisecracks.

Just to See What Happens

The competitions and elimination shows are latter-day Milgram experiments [1960s experiments that studied the relationship between obedience and authority] that place real people in artificial situations to *see what happens*. *The Apprentice* is Darwinism [referring to Charles Darwin's theory of survival of the fittest] set loose inside an entrepreneurial Habitrail. Post-9/11, *Survivor* became less a fantasy and more a metaphor for an imagined postapocalyptic future. What happens on these shows might be a Technicolor version of how we behave in real life, but so is most fiction. Creative endeavors—written, scripted, or produced—should be measured not by how literally they replicate actual life but by how effectively they render emotional truths. The best moments found on reality TV are unscriptable, or beyond the grasp of most scriptwriters. It's no coincidence that 2006's best scripted dramas—*The Wire*, HBO's multi-season epic of inner-city Baltimore; and *Children of Men*, Alfonso Cuarón's futuristic thriller—were studies in meticulously crafted "realness," deploying naturalistic dialogue, decentered and chaotic action, stutter-step pacing, and a reporter's eye for the telling detail. *The Wire's*

season and Cuarón's movie both ended on semi-resolved nov-
elistic notes, scorning the tendency in current television and
cinema toward easy narrative closure. Watching them only
threw into higher relief the inability of so much other scripted
product to get beyond stock characterizations and pat narrative.

For all the snobbism in the doc [documentary] community, reality TV has actually contributed to the recent boom in
documentary filmmaking. The most successful docs of recent
vintage have broken through in part by drawing heavily from
reality television's bag of tricks, dropping the form's canonical
insistence on pure observation. In *Fahrenheit 9/11*, [film-
maker] Michael Moore brings an Army recruiter with him to
confront legislators and urge them to enlist their children in
the Iraq War effort. In *Bowling for Columbine*, Moore takes
children who were shot at Columbine [High School in 1999]
to a Kmart, where they ask for a refund on the bullets that are
still lodged in their bodies. Of course, Moore's never been a
doc purist. *TV Nation*, his short-lived 1994 television series,
prefigured a long line of gonzo reality, from *Joe Millionaire* to
Punk'd. Having the Serbian ambassador sing along to the Bar-
ney theme song ("I love you, you love me") while statistics
about the number of Bosnians killed during the breakup of
Yugoslavia appeared on the screen was not only ur-reality
[i.e., foundational reality]; it was ur-Borat [title character in
satirical documentary about a journalist from Kazakhstan reporting on the United States]. And speaking of talking animals, *March of the Penguins* turned stunning footage of mat-
ing and migrating penguins into an utterly contrived Antarctic
version of *Love Story*.

The resistance to reality TV ultimately comes down to
snobbery, usually of the generational variety. People under 30,
in my experience, tend to embrace this programming; they're
happy to be entertained, never mind the purity of conception.
As an unapologetic producer of reality shows, I'm obviously

biased, but I also know that any genre that provokes such howls of protest is doing something interesting.

> *"Can the rest of us afford to live in a society constantly auditioning to make an ass of itself on TV?"*

Reality Television Debases Society

Jonah Goldberg

Jonah Goldberg is an author, columnist, and editor at large of the National Review. *In the following viewpoint, he argues that the popularity of reality television has functioned to accelerate the moral decline of America and has helped to create a society that values celebrity more than old-fashioned values.*

As you read, consider the following questions:

1. What reality show contestants does Goldberg list as worst-case examples?

2. What did the British historian Arnold Toynbee argue about civilizations, according to the author?

3. How does Goldberg define "ecumenical niceness"?

Culturally, this has been the decade [2000–2009] of the reality show. And what do we have to show for it? Not much more than the contestants themselves.

Reality Contestants Prove the Point

Survey the wreckage. Richard Hatch, the first *Survivor* champion, was just released from prison (he didn't pay taxes on his winnings). The marriage of the Octoparents [parents of eight children], Jon and Kate [Gosselin], is a shambles. Richard and Mayumi Heene were so desperate to land a reality series, they concocted an enormous hoax, convincing the country their child had been carried away in a balloon. Michaele and Tareq Salahi tried to claw their way onto the sure-to-be-hideous series *Real Housewives of D.C.* by brazening their way into a state dinner. And alleged wife-killer Ryan Jenkins, a contestant on two VH1 shows, is a stark reminder that fame is not a reflection of good character.

Which brings us to *Jersey Shore*. The show, which just started airing on MTV, follows a gaggle of barely literate bridge-and-tunnel steakheads and slatterns as they spend their summer at "the greatest meat market in the world." One of the absurdly tanned gibbons goes by the moniker "the Situation" because it gives him the excuse to ask women, "Do you love the Situation?" as he lifts his shirt to show off his washboard abs. Even if they all put their heads together, it's doubtful they could beat a carnival chicken at Tic-Tac-Toe.

In a teaser for this week's [December 2009] episode, one of the girls is punched in the face at a bar. But, after "consulting with experts on the issue of violence," MTV announced it wouldn't show the actual assault. While I can't fault the decision, it is kind of funny. The producers see nothing wrong with glorifying drunken idiocy and moral buffoonery in every episode, but they "responsibly" draw the line at physical violence because MTV is loath to promote reckless behavior.

Uh huh.

When the not-so-hidden cameras catch one of the girls cheating on her boyfriend with a housemate sporting a pierced you-know-what, that's just pure entertainment. "You have your penis pierced. I love it," the drunken vamp exclaims.

Don't get me wrong; it's great television. But gladiatorial games would be great TV, too.

A Crisis of Conscience

The *Los Angeles Times* reported the other day that the reality-show industry is suddenly having a crisis of conscience about its impact on the culture. That's nice to hear, but it's not nearly enough.

British historian Arnold Toynbee argued that civilizations thrive when the lower classes aspire to be like the upper classes, and they decay when the upper classes try to be like the lower classes. Looked at through this prism, it's hard not to see America in a prolonged period of decay.

It's not all bad news, to be sure. The elite minority's general acceptance of racial and sexual equality as important values has been a moral triumph. But not without costs. As part of this transformation, society has embraced what social scientist Charles Murray calls "ecumenical niceness." A core tenet of ecumenical niceness is that harsh judgments of the underclass—or people with underclass values—are forbidden. A corollary: People with old-fashioned notions of decency are fair game.

A Moral Vacuum

Long before the rise of reality shows, ecumenical niceness created a moral vacuum. Out-of-wedlock birth was once a great shame; now it's something of a happy lifestyle choice. The cavalier use of profanity was once crude; now it's increasingly conversational. Self-discipline was once a virtue; now self-expression is king.

Reality-show culture has thrived in that moral vacuum, accelerating the decay and helping to create a society in which celebrity is the new nobility. One senses that Richard Heene thought—maybe still thinks—that the way to make his kids proud of him was to land a reality show. Paris Hilton, famous for being famous thanks in part to a "reality" sex tape released days before her 2003 reality show *The Simple Life*, is now a cultural icon of no redeeming value whatsoever.

Whatever you think of what Toynbee and Murray would call the "proletarianization of the elites," one point is beyond dispute: The rich can afford moral lassitude more than the poor can. Hilton, heir to a hotel fortune, has life as simple as she wants it to be. [Professional golfer] Tiger Woods is surely a cad, but as a pure matter of economics, he can afford to be one.

The question is: Can the rest of us afford to live in a society constantly auditioning to make an ass of itself on TV?

> "Audiences find [courtroom television]
> entertaining and informative."

Courtroom Television
Shows Are Entertaining
and Educational

Lisa Respers France

Lisa Respers France is a contributor to CNN.com. In the follow-
ing viewpoint, she cites the popularity of courtroom television
shows in the United States and Canada, reporting their appeal
to be a mix of outspoken and engaging personalities and out-
landish litigants. France states that many viewers find the shows
both entertaining and educational.

As you read, consider the following questions:

1. According to Professor Steven Kohm, as cited by France,
   how often can viewers see courtroom television shows
   in Canada?

2. According to the author, what show received the first
   daytime Emmy for outstanding legal/courtroom program?

3. How many court shows have launched since the debut of *The People's Court*, according to France?

Shocking paternity results! Scorned lovers! Spouse swapping!

Once the exclusive fodder of soap operas and daytime talk shows, the titillating topics now are standard fare for men and women who wear robes and pound gavels.

Television courtroom shows are everywhere during the daytime, much to the delight of fans who can't get enough of judges taking litigants to task. They even cross the border.

"I've found that even in Canada, and we are feeding off of the American television stations here, you can pretty much get up at 8 o'clock in the morning and watch judging shows continually without interruption until 6 o'clock in the evening," said Steven Kohm, an assistant professor of Criminal Justice at the University of Winnipeg.

He has examined the appeal of courtroom programs in his academic research.

The Appeal of Courtroom TV

With its mix of small claims, outspoken judges and often outlandish litigants, the programming has become so popular that last year [2008] the National Academy of Television Arts and Sciences added outstanding legal/courtroom program to its Daytime Emmy Awards categories. The inaugural award went to *Cristina's Court*.

The format has come a long way since the early 1980s, when the granddaddy of them all, *The People's Court*, premiered, thrusting the show and its silver-haired arbiter of justice, Judge Joseph Wapner, into the limelight.

Now a cadre of shows including *Judge Judy*, *Judge Joe Brown*, *Judge Alex*, and *Divorce Court* are keeping viewers tuned in for a daily dose of justice.

The People's Court, ruled over by Judge Marilyn Milian, is produced by Telepictures Productions (a division of the parent company that also owns CNN).

The show is the longest running of Telepictures' courtroom programming, which includes *Judge Mathis* and newcomer *Judge Jeanine Pirro*.

Court TV Is Personality Driven

Hilary Estey McLoughlin, president of Telepictures Productions, said 24 court shows have launched since the debut of *The People's Court*. Thirteen of those are no longer on the air, she said.

From a business perspective, she said, such shows are affordable to produce and audiences find them entertaining and informative.

"When you look at the daytime environment, it is largely driven by distinctive personalities and compelling storytelling and court shows have both," she said.

Judge Greg Mathis recently celebrated a decade on the air.

Known for his "gang to gavel" background, having risen from a troubled childhood to Michigan District Court judge, Mathis said he believes shows like his help educate viewers about the legal system.

"I hear that all the time in the community, that they've learned so much," he said "They know what evidence to bring into court and they quote the law to their friends and family. In my observation, I would call that bootleg lawyering."

Critics Find Shows Unrealistic

Nancy B. Rapoport couldn't disagree more. The shows, with their bombastic jurists, are not realistic, said Rapoport, whose title—Gordon Silver Professor of Law at the University of Nevada, Las Vegas' William S. Boyd School of Law—could fill the docket sheet.

"They so don't behave the way real judges do, that for me it's like nails on a chalkboard," she said. "Real judges, except for the ones that end up getting disciplined, don't on an unprovoked basis yell at litigants. They try to uphold the dignity and decorum of the court."

Kohm, the Canadian professor, said the shows are theatrical examples of the tradition of crime and punishment: Those who exhibit bad behavior are publicly reprimanded, in some cases very dramatically.

"I think there's a long-standing belief, certainly in the American context, in this notion of do-it-yourself justice," Kohm said. "The idea that you can take your problems to a court and have a fair hearing in front of an objective third party is really embedded in the American ideal of democracy."

Court TV Teaches Valuable Lessons

Mary Ann Cooper has followed the programming for years and has written about *Divorce Court* for *TV Week*, an industry trade magazine.

Cooper said that while she doesn't believe TV court shows are making viewers more law savvy, she does believe they may be teaching lessons of fairness and personal responsibility.

With their public airing of dirty laundry and bad behavior, the programs will continue to be rubbernecked on the highway of reality television, Cooper predicts.

"In many cases, it's like the appeal of a train wreck," she said. "People are watching, in some cases, people getting their heads handed to them and are captivated."

> *"Syndicated courtroom shows . . . may mislead the common viewer into believing that the shows accurately represent the American justice system."*

Courtroom Television Shows Present a Distorted View of the American Legal System

Erika Lane

Erika Lane is a medical malpractice lawyer in New York City. In the following viewpoint, she argues that although syndicated courtroom television shows may be entertaining for viewers, they often do not accurately portray what happens in litigation proceedings and misrepresent what a judge is able to do in the courtroom.

As you read, consider the following questions:

1. According to Lane, are syndicated court television shows arbitration or litigation proceedings?

2. How do syndicated court television shows differ from litigation proceedings, according to the author?

Erika Lane, "Reality of Courtroom Television Shows," *Georgetown Journal of Legal Ethics*, v. 20, 779, Summer 2007. Reprinted with permission of the publisher, Georgetown Journal of Ethics © 2007.

3. What does Lane view as the dangers of the viewers' confusion or misperception of court television shows?

In the midst of the recent [2007] celebrity case involving the burial location of Anna Nicole Smith's body, it was not just the sudden tragic death of this well-known celebrity that had people gossiping. It was, rather, the unusual behavior of the judge hearing the case, Judge Larry Seidlin. Seidlin's bizarre comments and mockery of the dispute resembled, in the public's view, behavior common to what has become a major popular phenomenon in daytime television in America—syndicated courtroom television shows. Seemingly unprofessional and regarding the courtroom as an entertainment show, Judge Seidlin received significant criticism for his jokes, slang language, and what appeared to be a disregard for the integrity of the courtroom. In a society where approximately 8.5 million people watch syndicated courtroom shows daily, the line between what is a real arbitration or litigation proceeding and what is doctored on television and not an accurate portrayal of reality becomes so blurred that even our own judges seem to get confused about their role in the courtroom.

Given the presence of a television in nearly every household in America and the soaring popularity of reality television shows, Americans today are increasingly exposed to televised portrayals of our country's professional sectors as well as to "real" people with "real" stories. However, while reality shows provide significant entertainment to the public, they do not always accurately present the actual functioning of these sectors or the stories of their "actors." This carries the danger of confusing the public about what "reality" really is. Specifically, programs like syndicated courtroom shows (also referred to as "syndi-court" shows) may mislead the common viewer into believing that the shows accurately represent the American justice system. Syndicated courtroom programs take place in what appear to be real courtrooms, but are in fact simply televised arbitration dispute resolutions. The parties present their cases to the arbitrator (who looks like a "judge" to the viewer) and, within minutes, the arbitrator decides the outcome, usually with some form of moral reprimand to the parties, thereby providing substantial entertainment to the audience. . . .

The Nature of Syndicated Court Shows

While syndicated court shows are arbitration proceedings, they portray themselves to the public as litigation proceedings. By engaging in this inaccurate representation, syndi-court shows are neither typical arbitrations nor trials. Further, they mislead viewers to believe syndi-shows are accurate reflections of how our judicial system works. Such inaccurate portrayals carry with them the danger of confusing the public about their legal rights, about judges and the justice system, and about arbitration.

Syndicated court shows present themselves as real trials, involving real-life cases. The shows air for thirty minutes or an hour and the syndi-judge hears two or four cases. In each case, the syndi-judge hears both sides of the dispute directly from the "litigants" (there are no attorneys involved) and, within minutes, decides the outcomes. The disputes revolve around family and domestic issues and do not involve large monetary awards. Usually, when giving his or her judgment, the syndi-judge will deliver a moral message or reprimand to the parties, expressing his or her personal views regarding their situations.

Creating a False Impression

Syndi-court shows appear as real courtroom settings. The judges enter the set, dressed in a robe, with a gavel in hand. A bailiff swears in the parties, and they each stand before the judge, who sits at a bench and hears their disputes. These props and tactics leave viewers with the impression that the show is a real courtroom trial.

While the audience of certain televised syndicated court-room programs may believe that these are real cases brought by "real people," these realistic qualities to the show really do not accurately reflect both typical arbitration proceedings and real trials. In a typical arbitration, an arbitrator who is either chosen by the parties or administered by a private organization privately resolves disputes. An arbitrator's decision is final and binding on the parties. Arbitration, intended to be an inexpensive and time-sensitive method of dispute resolution, does not require arbitrators to follow the *Federal Rules of Evidence* when resolving disputes. However, there are certain checks on arbitrators; the *Arbitrators Ethical Guidelines* encourage arbitrators to adhere to their ethical standards by prescribing that "the purpose of [the guidelines] is to provide basic guidance regarding ethical issues that may arise during or related to the arbitration process."

Similarities and Differences

While syndi-shows are arbitration proceedings and they do bear certain similarities to typical arbitrations, they ultimately do not portray themselves closely to arbitration proceedings. Similar to a typical arbitration, the parties agree in advance to resolve their disputes by the syndi-judge. Additionally, syndi-court shows' arbitration proceedings are short (each syndi-judge hears two disputes during a half hour time period). Furthermore, the syndi-judges' decisions are final and binding on the parties. Syndi-court arbitrations, however, do not take place in private settings, and they include moral messages rendered with the syndi-judges' final decisions. While an arbitrator in a private dispute resolution may voice his or her moral opinion, his or her moral judgment would only be heard by the parties to the dispute. In a syndi-court show, any harsh moral judgment rendered by a syndi-judge can be witnessed by millions of viewers. Such moral judgments are often harsh and delivered in ways that are not tolerated by the *Arbitrators*

Ethical Guidelines, yet syndi-judges are never sanctioned or reprimanded for harsh treatment of the parties. Furthermore, in typical arbitration proceedings, the arbitrator does not dress like a judge and hold a gavel. A bailiff does not swear the parties into the room and they do not have to rise before the arbitrator.

Unlike arbitration, litigation can be very costly and time-consuming. Practicing judges are bound by several rules and guidelines when deciding cases, including rules of evidence, rules of jurisdiction, rules of candor and conduct, and constitutional requirements (such as the Confrontation Clause); they [as attorney Christina Leb states,] "have checks upon how they do their job." Such checks may include an appeal process to question the validity of the judge's decision or ethical standards to which the judge must adhere. Litigation proceedings are also typically not private (they are open to the public) and judges are pro-appointed and not chosen by the parties. Litigation is less flexible than arbitration, as the parties cannot choose the process to hear the dispute (it is determined by procedural laws).

Using Props Effectively

While syndi-court shows resemble courtroom settings, they do not accurately represent litigation proceedings. Because they are really arbitrations, they do not portray adherence to rules of evidence, motions made by parties, and witnesses, although may be heard by the syndi-judge, are not sworn in. Even syndi-court judges admit to the shows' similarity to trials, without the details of what makes a trial a trial. For example, in an interview with [television host] Larry King, Judge Mills Lane admitted to Larry King's observation that, "it's sort of like Court TV without having to put up with all the extraneous objections and the like." The props on syndi-shows, including the gavel, the judge's robe, and the bailiff all give the impression that the disputes are trials, being decided by judges. Yet

Feel-Good Justice Porn

Instead of making us more responsible citizens, more inclined to rely on our own good judgment rather than public institutions, justice porn popularizes the idea that the court system is a legitimate venue for mending friendships, punishing moral (but not criminal) transgressions, and seeking inspirational hugs from stern but caring authority figures. At the same time, it positions judges as unquestionable authorities with unlimited power to scrutinize our lives.

Greg Beato, Reason, *January 2009.*

these props are all that the public sees and syndi-shows, as arbitration proceedings under the guise of trials, lack all that makes a trial a trial.

The Dangers of Fooling the Audience

There are dangers of misperception and confusion among the public that arise from the syndi-courts' misrepresentation of both arbitration and litigation. As syndi-court shows currently exist, the public may assume that syndi-courts are accurate representations of real trials and are not in fact, arbitration proceedings. In assuming syndi-shows are real trials, viewers might conclude that they need not seek the advice and aid of counsel, and that they can bring a limitless range of suits, no matter how frivolous (if so inexpensive and timely). This misconception may lead individuals to abuse or neglect their legal rights without even knowing it. Further, the parties themselves on the syndi-shows may neglect their legal rights without knowing it. Parties who appear on syndi-shows are typically uneducated about the judicial system and overly eager about appearing on television; they may not necessarily realize when a syndi-judge acts inappropriately towards them. This factor combined with the fact that parties sign agreements consenting not to seek redress against a syndi-judge makes them vulnerable to being exploited on public television.

Syndi-courts also risk confusing the public into believing that syndi-judges are reflective of actual judges or of arbitrators. Viewers, after seeing harsh treatment towards parties on syndi-shows, may form negative views of judges and of the judicial system as a whole. They may not realize that in typical legal proceedings, such behavior is frowned upon and even prohibited. Yet even with a negative view of judges, viewers still risk relying on that perception of judges and entering litigation or arbitration with false expectations of what the process will be like. For instance, the State of California Commission on Judicial Performance, a state organization that investigates judicial misconduct, frequently receives complaints from California citizens about disappointment that judges were entirely different than what was expected, based on viewers' perceptions from syndi-shows. This false expectation can lead to confusion of the parties once involved in litigation or arbitration and could lead them to misunderstand their legal rights or the judicial process.

Confusing the Law with Television

Furthermore, syndi-courts' representations as real courtrooms also pose a potential risk of confusing the public between what may be actual law and what may be a manipulation of the law to rationalize an individual's own moral judgment. Many syndicated court shows deliver moral messages, and while they may be positive messages that the public should value, it could create confusion resulting in the individuals acting in ways they believe are protected by the law, when in fact those actions are merely consistent with an individual arbitrator's personal opinion, articulated in a specific dispute.

If syndicated courtrooms explained to the public in a clear disclaimer that they are not representative of our judicial system, perhaps the problem would improve. These shows, however, do just the opposite by implying that they are the benchmark of our legal system all through unreadable disclaimers, settings, costumes, and props.

❙ *"[Prison television] is educational."*

Prison Television Educates Viewers About the Prison Experience

James Parker

James Parker is a contributing editor for the Atlantic. *In the following viewpoint, he explores the appeal of prison television shows to the American public. Parker concludes that shows like MSNBC's* Lockup *are educational and a chance to satisfy one's curiosity about the prison experience.*

As you read, consider the following questions:

1. According to the author, when did MSNBC start airing its *Lockup* series?

2. What was Jeremy Bentham's planned "Panopticon," according to Parker?

3. What does the author believe is the most instructional of the *Lockup* series?

A few tips for the newly incarcerated: tattoo ink can be mixed up from the soot of burned baby oil. Look out for the bacteria in the home brew (it is, after all, just rotted fruit). Should a guard confiscate your headphones during a cell shakedown, seek the earliest opportunity to throw a cup of urine on him. Something to read during heroin withdrawal? Try Viktor Frankl's *Man's Search for Meaning.* And if, for your own safety, you desire to be placed in Administrative Segregation, you might consider ratting out the leader of a white-supremacist gang.

I should say that my observations are not derived from experience. Unless watching television counts as experience, which I don't think it does. Yet. At any rate, I've never been to prison. These jewels of inmate savvy were gleaned, rather, during the many edifying hours I have spent in front of MSNBC's *Lockup,* the documentary franchise that since 2000 has been sending its film crews scuttling through the penal facilities of America, and lately the world. *Lockup* was followed by *Lockup: Raw,* then by *Lockup: Extended Stay* and *Lockup: World Tour*—if you want to know about conjugal visits in San Quentin [State Penitentiary in California], racial politics at Wabash Valley [Correctional Facility in Indiana], or what a Serbian execution chamber looks like, executive producer Rasha Drachkovitch and his team have got the goods.

A Voyeur's Heaven

"Due to *mature* subject matter," the emphatic deep-sea voice warns at the start of each episode, "viewer *discretion* is advised." And indeed the subject matter is very mature—has been maturing, one might say, since the book of Genesis. Discretion, on the other hand—well, we're way past that. Drachkovitch's cameras get everywhere, into everything, fully licensed by the Age of Access, and we go with them. Here are the convicts plotting their plots, flooding their cells, doing their chin-ups, chiseling away at their shivs and shanks; here is the dead-eyed felon, and here the tittering psychopath. Here is Fleece Johnson, a woolly-hatted veteran of Kentucky State Penitentiary, gravely recalling the good old days: "In this prison, booty was more important than food. Booty. A man's butt. I'm serious! Booty, havin' some booty, was more important than drinkin' water, man."

Sensational? Sort of exploitative? Intermittently debasing? Check, check, and check again. But *Lockup* keeps going, into unexpected zones of sympathy and catharsis. Here too is Leon Benson, doing 60 years for murder and locked down 23 hours a day in the Secured Housing Unit (SHU) at Wabash Valley Correctional Facility, reciting through the meal slot, or "pieflap," in his cell door his rewrite of *Macbeth*: "You read my eyes like parables ... The sky has the residues of sunlight, but it's fading away like butter on corn bread." The words resound metallically. Down the hallway, through another pieflap, a fellow participant in Wabash's "Shakespeare in the SHU" program voices his appreciation: "I really like the metaphor you use. 'You read my eyes like parables.' Right? Man, that's almost something like Shakespeare himself would write." Chris "Pain" Lashbrook (eight years at Limon Correctional Facility, in Colorado, for auto theft and burglary), a pale behemoth with injury in his eyes and tattoos spidering up from his neckline, sits across the table from his primary abuser, the chief architect of his ruin. "The slaps and kicks turned into punches and head butts, broken nose, cigarettes being put out on me ... From the age of 7 to 11, I probably felt every piece of physical abuse a kid can feel." But he loves his father, and the two men are talking, very softly, about playing guitar. "I've been getting into the Foo Fighters, stuff like that," says Lashbrook Sr. "Still playing the Coldplay?" his son asks. "Yep, still doin' some Coldplay."

Prison TV as Reality TV

Hands up, who can tell me where reality TV first entered the universe? Was it with Buñuel's *Exterminating Angel* (dinner-party guests trapped in a room), or the *Stanford Prison Experiment*? *Lockup* has its elements of reality-ness: no *Big Brother* housemate, after all, was ever so poked and prodded and surveilled as your average convict.

> It is obvious that, in all these instances, the more constantly the persons to be inspected are under the eyes of the persons who should inspect them, the more perfectly will the purpose of the establishment have been attained.

So wrote [English philosopher] Jeremy Bentham in 1787, about his planned "Panopticon"—a temple of correction, circular in design, whose inmates would be exposed to an unsleeping scrutiny. The thing was never built, thank God, but as the *Lockup* cameras sniff out the grimmest intimacies of prison life, and rush toward its flash points, it seems proper to ask ourselves what, in this case, "the purpose" might be.

The Appeal of Prison TV

Wherein lies the attraction of prison TV? Men in particular can watch it like the Home Shopping Network, with a bright and endless curiosity. With prison, there are always ultimate questions involved, of course, and ultimate destinations—the abyss of perdition, the great glass elevator of redemption—but more immediately thrilling to the couch potato, I think, is just the vastly bummed-out texture of prison life: the din of hard surfaces, hard voices, hard lights; the big dude hanging heavy forearms over the back of a chair as he tells his tale; the hellishly perfected torsos around the weights bench, where a scowling lifter struts like the creature in William Blake's *The Ghost of a Flea*; the cafeteria slop; the dismal, travestied politics; the top dog on the tier, who in passing plucks a baseball hat from somebody's head and sets it conclusively on his own. Tickled, scarified, the unincarcerated viewer thanks his lucky stars and solemnly wonders after what fashion he might, if it came to it, do his own time.

Prison TV Is Educational

And beyond that, *Lockup* is educational. The most instructive parts of the franchise are generally to be found in the shows subtitled *Extended Stay*. Whereas *Lockup: Raw* and *Lockup: World Tour* bounce from prison to prison, hectic compendia of horrors and enlightenments, *Extended Stay* digs in for months at a time in one location. Prisons are tiny totalitarian states, each with its own kinks and caprices, and the long-haul format gives Drachkovitch's crew time to tease out the idiosyncrasies of a given facility—to taste, as it were, the time that is being done there. At Limon, for example, under the regime of Warden Travis Trani, two facts are notable. First, sex offenders are obliged to take their chances in the general population. Second, in the wake of an attack on a staff member, that population's freedom of movement and association has been severely curtailed. Violence is down overall, but the policy has received predictably mixed notices. "When you separate dogs like that," grumbles one inmate over a game of cards, "then they bark. But if you got 'em all together, everyone knows their place in the pack. They don't get out of line." "You been watching *Dog Whisperer* too much," somebody responds. The inmate is unabashed: "Just like *Dog Whisperer*. For real. It's true."

Perennially enthralling, too, are the prisoners with whom it appears that nothing can be done—the literally incorrigible, or those who have been bashed into a pure state of defiance, beyond the last straw, beyond everything. "I am getting f---ing *tired* of f---ing with you," complains Kevin Blanco, serving 13 years for attempted murder, to a guard at the Penitentiary of New Mexico. In solitary confinement, Blanco is a one-man band of disobedience, tossing around his bodily fluids, refusing to "cuff up," and "taking hostage" the small spaces that are available to him—his "rec pen," for example, with its shining clouds of razor wire and its lonely basketball hoop. Simply by declining to vacate this cage when asked, Blanco can trigger "standard extraction protocol," and a team of guards gruntingly straps itself into vests and helmets. "Go get your goon squad," he says. "Go get your gas, and c'mon." "There's not much more that we can do to him, as far as disciplinary sanctions," concedes Sergeant Arturo Suazo.

Jerry Weir, a former member of NAMBLA [North American Man/Boy Love Association] with a scrunched, hobbity face, doing time at Limon for sexual exploitation of a child, seems more cooperative. "I'm gonna do," he explains to a stoically attentive corrections officer, "whatever I have to do to let you help myself get what I want to help myself. Does that make sense?" "No," the officer says. And pictures of children *will* keep finding their way into Weir's cell. Busted. Back in the hole. "He's not never gonna catch on," predicts a sergeant. Kevin Blanco, meanwhile, having taken his rec pen hostage, is perched on top of that basketball hoop with an air of eremitic remoteness. All measures, all efforts, have failed. The pepper spray didn't bother him; the tear gas was dispersed by a friendly breeze; three nonlethal shotgun rounds have caromed ineffectually off his ribcage. "I'll come down," he announces, "if you shoot me one more time." *Clang!* goes a round into the hoop's metal frame. "All right," says Blanco. And down he comes.

> *"Reality-based crime programmes present highly-edited versions of reality, while claiming to present the unadulterated truth."*

Prison Television Offers a Skewed View of the Prison Experience

Dawn K. Cecil and Jennifer L. Leitner

Dawn K. Cecil is associate professor and Jennifer L. Leitner a law student at the University of South Florida. In the following viewpoint, they analyze how US prison shows like MSNBC's Lockup *depict prison life. Cecil and Leitner conclude that the series offers a heavily edited version of real life in prison.*

As you read, consider the following questions:

1. According to the authors, how many adults are in prison in the United States?

2. According to Cecil and Leitner, how many televised documentaries featuring prisons were broadcast on US cable television during a recent six-month period?

Dawn K. Cecil and Jennifer L. Leitner, "Unlocking the Gates: An Examination of *MSNBC Investigates—Lockup*," *The Howard Journal of Criminal Justice*, v. 48, 2, May 2009. Copyright © 2009 by The Howard Journal of Criminal Justice. Reproduced by permission.

3. What is the top prison show on cable television in the United States, according to Cecil and Leitner?

In the United States there are more than 1.5 million adults in prison. Despite the fact that incarceration touches the lives of so many, the general public has limited knowledge of prisons. Lacking firsthand experience with the prison system, most people's impressions of these institutions are derived from the images they receive. According to [R. Surette in *Media, Crime, and Criminal Justice,*]: 'It is a tenet of social constructionism that the more remote the subject, the more the public perception of it will be shaped by media imagery'; thus media images are critical to the public's perception of these institutions.

In the US there is a growing number of televised prison documentaries, which purport to offer a real look into prison life. While research has focused on prison films and, to some extent, televised prison dramas, little attention has been paid to the reality-based media images. This article seeks to explore how a televised documentary series, *MSNBC Investigates—Lockup*, depicts American prisons. In doing so, several questions are posed. First, how do televised documentaries portray prison? Second, is this portrayal accurate and representative? Finally, how do the producers frame the issue of imprisonment?

Prisons in the Media

Images of prisons can be found throughout the media; some of these images are fictional, while others are reality-based. Most of the literature on these images of prison focuses on films, while some of it refers to the less common televised prison drama. While rooted in fantasy, prison films and televised dramas are marketed as true depictions of life behind bars. Overall, media images of prison are rare; therefore, the influence of these fictionalised images cannot be underestimated.

Images of prison are also found in the news and in reality-based crime programmes on television, although both are relatively rare in comparison to prison films. Since uncommon events such as riots and escapes are considered newsworthy, news stories about the prison system are scarce. [In *Popular Culture, Crime, and Justice,* Steven M.] Chermak found that only 17% of the crime stories in his study covered correctional institutions. The low occurrence of these news stories may explain the dearth of research on how prisons are depicted in the news. . . . What is known is that negative correctional stories are more prominent than positive ones. These stories tend to focus on problems of the prison system through stories of the system failing to protect the public, pursuing improper goals, and corruption and brutality within the system.

Prison Documentaries

Real-life images of prison are not limited to those in the news media. Documentaries also offer insight into the prison system; however, to date there has not been a lot of research on this topic. [Jamie] Bennett examined Rex Bloomstein's British documentaries on prison, while [Dawn K.] Cecil examined American documentaries featuring women in prison. Surette states that very few prison documentaries have received widespread play. This observation may explain the lack of attention to the content of these documentaries, however, the changing nature of television programming has changed the structure of documentaries. Over time, many of these televised documentaries took on elements of entertainment-style programming in order to draw in viewers; this technique has become known as infotainment. Surette argues that the correctional system is not a significant topic in this genre due to the fact that prison films market themselves as accurate depictions and prison administrators do not have any incentive to co-operate with the filming of these shows. However, during a recent six-month period, over 50 televised documentaries featuring prisons were recorded on American cable television.

One particular series to offer insight into the prison system airs on the 24-hour cable news station MSNBC. Their series, *MSNBC Investigates—Lockup*, hereafter referred to as *Lockup*, is an example of televised images of prison from the infotainment perspective. Each episode begins with a warning to the viewers, followed by: 'There are 2 million people behind bars in America. We open the gates'. Unlocking the gates suggests an all-access look into these institutions. Purporting to offer secrets of life behind bars by examining real prisons across the US, this show has the potential to overshadow the images received from fictional accounts of prison. Yet, the nature of the genre itself means the line between fact and fiction is blurred.

Infotainment Programmes and Frames

Viewers of prison films and televised dramas recognise on some level that these accounts of prison life are fictionalised, even if they are unsure of which elements have been subjected to interpretation and shaped by the creative process. However, when watching reality-based programmes the audience may not take into consideration the process used to create the final product. Reality-based crime programmes present highly-edited versions of reality, while claiming to present the unadulterated truth.

A major component viewers may not consider is the editing process. While a valid consideration for all reality-based crime programming, it is especially pertinent to those presenting prison life. Producers are required to adhere to the wishes of prison administrators, who must maintain control of the institution and ensure the safety of those involved. Once the film crew leaves the prison the producers will edit the images to create a story. The story that is presented depends on how the issue being presented is framed.

Prisons Featured on MSNBC Investigates—Lockup*

Name (year produced)	Location	Security Level	Gender of Population	Inmate Population
Anamosa State Penitentiary (2005)	Iowa	Maximum	Male	1,300
Brushy Mountain Correctional Complex (2006)	Tennessee	Maximum	Male	560
Return to Corcoran (2005)	California	Maximum	Male	5,000
Elayn Hunt Correctional Center (2005)	Louisiana	Maximum	Male	2,100
Folsom State Prison (2000)	California	Maximum	Male	4,000
Holman Correctional Facility (2006)	Alabama	Maximum	Male	1,000
Indiana State Prison (2006)	Indiana	Maximum	Male	2,000
Iowa State Penitentiary (2006)	Iowa	Maximum	Male	566
Kentucky State Penitentiary (2005)	Kentucky	Maximum	Male	900
Penitentiary of New Mexico (2005)	New Mexico	Maximum	Male	800
North Carolina Correctional Institution for Women (2005)	North Carolina	Maximum	Female	1,100
Return to Pelican Bay (2005)	California	Maximum	Male	3,489

continued

Prisons Featured on MSNBC Investigates—Lockup* [CONTINUED]

Name (year produced)	Location	Security Level	Gender of Population	Inmate Population
Riverbend Maximum Security Institution (2005)	Tennessee	Maximum	Male	700
San Quentin State Prison (2000)	California	Maximum	Male	5,850
Stateville Correctional Center (2000)	Illinois	Maximum	Male	2,600
Utah State Prison (2005)	Utah	Maximum	Both	4,000
Wabash Valley Correctional Facility (2005)	Indiana	Maximum	Male	2,200

Note: *Each episode is produced by 44 Blue Productions.

TAKEN FROM: Dawn K. Cecil and Jennifer L. Leitner, "Unlocking the Gates," *The Howard Journal of Criminal Justice*, May 2009.

Frames [, states Gaye Tuchman,] 'are the focus, a parameter or boundary, for discussing a particular event. Frames focus on what will be discussed, how it will be discussed, and above all, how it will not be discussed'. According to Tuchman, frames are influenced, in part, by prior frames. The frames used determine the nature of the coverage, since producers will discard information that does not fit into these prescribed frames. Cecil found that producers of women-in-prison programmes drew from notorious 'babes-behind-bars' films and other media stereotypes of females to frame the issue through the lenses of sex, violence, and motherhood, thereby failing to address some of the main issues facing women in prison. Similarly, frames used in other prison documentaries are most likely based on those previously used, thereby limited the view of imprisonment presented.

MSNBC Investigates—Lockup

Lockup debuted in 2000, originally featuring ten one-hour long documentaries. Each episode focuses on one prison, offering insight into life within that institution. According to Sarah Paoge [in 2007], an executive with 44 Blue Productions, the purpose of the programme is 'to give an unbiased view of a day in the life of the prison'. Producers try to speak to everyone from inmates to treatment and custody staff, as well as prison administrators. Each hour-long episode is filmed over the course of eight consecutive days. The biggest hurdle is convincing administrators to allow them access to the institution. According to Sarah Paoge:

> [t]his can take a lot of time and convincing, even with the great reputation we have developed over the years. Often times the prisons and jails feel that our presence will be too much of an interruption to the daily operation of their facility, regardless of how big or small our camera crew is.

Despite these challenges, 31 episodes of the original *Lockup* series have aired on MSNBC.

Currently there are several different prison documentary series airing on cable television in the United States. There are several reasons why *Lockup* was selected for this study. First, it is both a popular and an award winning programme. It is currently rated as the top prison show on cable television in the United States and in 2001 won a film and documentary award for one of its episodes (44 Blue Productions 2008). In addition, it was the first series of its kind to air in the United States and is currently one of the longest running televised prison documentary series. Similar series have subsequently been added to the line-up on other cable television stations in the United States, including *Lockdown* on the National Geographic Channel and *Inside*, a short-lived series on Court TV, both of which debuted in 2007. *Lockup*'s popularity has led to the development of two spin-off series currently airing on MSNBC. The first, *Lockup Extended Stay*, features several episodes focusing on San Quentin [in California], Holman [in Alabama], and Corcoran [in California] Prisons. The second, *Lockup Raw*, features never-before-seen footage from previous episodes of the original *Lockup* series. Since these two spin-offs are relatively new and have a slightly different focus from the original *Lockup* series, episodes from these two programmes were not included in this study.

Periodical Bibliography

The following articles have been selected to supplement the diverse views presented in this chapter.

Joe Dugan — "Lessons in Lending: Get Back to Reality, Not Reality TV," *Daily Record*, July 2, 2010.

Esquire — "What's Wrong with a Little Bigotry?" May 2010.

Nancy Franklin — "Frenemy Territory," *New Yorker*, April 21, 2008.

Raina Kelley — "Reality TV Hates Women," *Newsweek*, June 3, 2009.

Charles Leroux — "Inexpensive Courtroom Shows Keep Luring Viewers," *Denver Post*, December 23, 2008.

Joanne Ostrow Limon — "Prison Is Doing Some Time on 'Lockup,'" *Denver Post*, November 20, 2009.

Jeremy W. Peters — "When Reality TV Gets Too Real," *New York Times*, October 8, 2007.

James Poniewozik — "What's Right with Reality TV," *Time*, February 22, 2010.

Ramin Setoodeh — "Reality TV Gets Real," *Newsweek*, December 13, 2007.

Adam Sternbergh — "Are We Running Out of Talent? Reality TV's New Crisis?" *New York*, March 15, 2010.

Lane Wallace — "Is Reality TV Torture?" *Atlantic*, August 7, 2009.

Edward Wyatt — "Television Fledgling Keeps It Real," *New York Times*, July 26, 2009.

Susan Young — "Mark Burnett Raises Reality TV Genre," *Variety*, July 7, 2009.

OPPOSING
VIEWPOINTS®
SERIES

CHAPTER 3

How Does Television Advertising Affect Society?

Chapter Preface

In recent years, controversy has erupted over the airing of advocacy ads on prime-time network television. Advocacy ads are a special form of advertising that advocate for a certain point of view or publicize a certain opinion on controversial public issues. They can be directed at specific targets, like an individual or company; or they can be meant for more general targets, such as a business industry, a political ideology, or the media. Advocacy ads can be funded by businesses, special-interest groups, political parties, and even individuals who want to publicize their points of view and garner support for them.

Advocacy ads have a long history in the US media. In newspapers and magazines, companies, groups, or individuals would buy a full-page ad and use it to advance their views. In one example, a private citizen bought a two-page ad in the *New York Times* in the 1960s to publicize his peace plan for ending the war in Vietnam. In another example of advocacy advertising, Mobil Oil Company bought air time on NBC to broadcast ads arguing for the need for offshore oil drilling in 1974. When ABC and CBS turned down the ads because of the controversy surrounding them, Mobil then bought a full-page ad in a number of newspapers and provided a transcript of the commercial.

In 2010, controversy exploded when CBS decided to air a thirty-second spot from the Christian advocacy group Focus on the Family during the Super Bowl. In the ad, Pam Tebow, the mother of celebrated University of Florida football quarterback Tim Tebow, recounts how she ignored doctors' advice to consider aborting her son, Tim, when medical problems plagued her pregnancy in 1987 while visiting the Philippines. Tim was born healthy and went on to win the 2007 Heisman Trophy for his play at Florida.

Pro-choice advocacy groups criticized CBS's decision to air the ad. They felt that the Super Bowl, with its heightened viewership, was an inappropriate time to air a controversial ad. Others felt that it revealed CBS's political ideology: in 2004, after CBS rejected an ad by the United Church of Christ (UCC) highlighting its tolerant and welcoming stance toward gay worshippers, critics viewed the network as biased toward conservative policies and against more liberal ones.

CBS responded to the criticism by revealing that after the controversy of 2004 it had reviewed its policies on advocacy ads. Therefore, the decision to air the Tebow ad reflected this revised policy, which would consider responsibly produced ads from all groups, no matter the issue or ideology. Under that new policy, CBS would have aired the UCC ad if it had been submitted for consideration in 2010. The network also pointed out that it had run ads with diverse views on other controversial issues such as the health-care debate, climate change, and energy policy.

Advocacy ads are considered a long-standing feature of the US advertising landscape. Many people argue that they are protected by the free-speech right of the First Amendment to the US Constitution. Yet, it is also acknowledged that the networks have to consider their own standards and practices and develop consistent criteria for accepting and airing such often controversial advertising. The debate over advocacy ads is just one covered in the viewpoints in the following chapter, which examines the effect of television advertising on individuals and society.

> *"What is allowed to air on television is simply a reflection of what society deems to be acceptable—it's a sign of the times."*

Television Ads Reflect Society

Nathan Hoofnel

Nathan Hoofnel is a contributor to Helium, a knowledge cooperative where professional journalists, freelance writers, and researchers can contribute articles on a multitude of topics to share with online readers. In the following viewpoint, he argues that television ads reflect the more liberal standards of our era and are tame compared to the lyrics of popular music. Hoofnel points out that the Federal Communications Commission protects children from the most dangerous material, and the rest falls under the protection of free speech.

As you read, consider the following questions:

1. What does the First Amendment of the US Constitution state, according to Hoofnel?

2. According to the author, when did the FCC start regulating communications in the United States?

3. What issues does Hoofnel believe are more important to the United States?

In today's world, television is simply a reality—a big reality. The media takes a large role in shaping our nation's culture. The average United States citizen spends hours in front of the television every day, and many of these viewers are quite young. Advertisers seem to keep pushing the boundaries in their television advertisements, and as a result some of these advertisements are progressively becoming more controversial. The question at hand is whether or not something should be done about these advertisements, and if so, what? The answer to this question is already written in black and white; the issue was settled on March 4, 1789 when the Constitution of the United States of America was put into action after being ratified by enough states. Because we are a nation of laws and ostensibly strict adherence to those laws, controversial advertising on television is within the boundaries of the Constitution and must be permitted so long as it meets Federal Communications Commission's (F.C.C.) requirements and regulations.

Some Regulation Is Needed

The first amendment of the U.S. Constitution specifically states, "Congress shall make no law respecting an establishment of religion, or prohibiting the free exercise thereof; or abridging the freedom of speech, or of the press." As one sees, if an attempt to ban controversial television advertising was made, numerous problems would instantly present themselves, the first of which is that we'd be violating our rights to freedom of speech. Companies use advertisements as a means to boost their sales—it's their way of speaking. They are guaranteed the right to speak freely and that is not up for debate in this country, although I do think that a line can be drawn between controversial advertisements and downright obscenities. Where the aforementioned line is to be drawn is another question altogether, a question better left to the F.C.C. to answer. The F.C.C. has been regulating communications of various forms here in the United States since 1934. It's understood that some guidelines, rules and regulations must be put into place on the airwaves and sound waves or there will be those who take things to the extreme; the next thing you know you'll have pornography on daytime television instead of children's cartoons. It's the F.C.C.'s job to make sure these things don't happen. They are the watchdogs of the airwaves.

According to federal law, obscene programming can't be aired at all, and strict regulations are placed on what can air during certain hours of the day. For example, fewer advertisements are allowed to air during certain hours when children are likely to be a majority of the viewing audience. In determining what should be considered obscene, they use contemporary community standards. It seems to be the nature of society that, as time goes on, more things are considered acceptable. I'm sure we're all familiar with the 1956 episode of the Ed Sullivan Show which featured the rock 'n' roller, Elvis Presley, as the musical guest. Mr. Sullivan didn't think the leg shaking was appropriate for television and decided to only show Elvis from the waist up. Obviously, times have changed and the status quo is getting more and more liberated with what's acceptable on the television. In the years to come as society becomes more and more tolerant of what's acceptable, will the F.C.C. allow pretty much anything to air? Though this seems to be the logical course of events, I don't think we need to worry ourselves about daytime cartoons full of graphic violence, nudity and profanity. The natural desire to protect our children will intervene and prevent this from occurring. For those who may disagree, just take a look back through history; even in the earliest of recorded times parents have cared for their young and taken extreme measures to protect their children. This characteristic is engrained in the human and is not likely to change.

Protecting Children from Indecency

Here's a world to imagine: a society in which very strict regulations are placed on what can be shown or said on television. One is sure to dream of ridiculous lawsuits when pondering this hypothetical society; these lawsuits would not only be ridiculous, but they'd be detrimental to the economy and bring about a whole wave of junk trial lawyers looking to capitalize off of anything they can. When the gray area of what's allowed on television is too broad, we are sure to encounter many problems. Besides, in a free-market society, those companies [choosing] to use poor taste or obscenities in their advertising methods would surely create their own demise. But to protect the viewers, especially the young viewers, I firmly believe in placing some level of regulation [on] television broadcasting.

Another reality regarding children is that we can only protect them so much. In today's age of the informational revolution, children have such a wide variety of sources to view or hear potentially obscene material that it's extremely difficult to protect them from all of these. In effect, it would be pointless and futile and place such rigid regulations on television advertising because what they'll see on television isn't half as bad as what they'll hear on their friend's iPod. Some parents may be naive to this. If this is the case I encourage these parents to listen to some of today's most popular rap and hip-hop stars' songs. Lyrics that promote drug use, violence and disrespect of women are being memorized by children of all ages. The lyrics of these so-called "artists" are far more dangerous than even the most controversial of today's television advertisements. The frightening part of this unfortunate cultural circumstance is the rate at which the popularity of these vulgar and obscene rappers is spreading.

TV Ads Are a Sign of the Times

The European Union has a ban on tobacco and prescription medicines advertisements and limitations on alcohol advertisements. It seems that they are trying to protect their citizens from dangerous habits, like smoking tobacco and drinking alcohol. Do these methods really work? Perhaps to some degree, but personally, I believe the decision to smoke should be up to the individual; it's not the responsibility of the government. Other than the aforementioned items, the regulations are generally the same; it seems that internationally, there are some lines that just aren't to be crossed—these are universal standards of decency. The bottom line is that even with the stricter regulations in Europe, they still aren't producing greater results in the areas forbidden the right to advertise. Even with their governmental protection (the forbiddance of particular types of advertisements) they still have a significantly higher percentage of smokers than we do here in the United States. Overall, things in the United States are far from perfect. We have issues to be concerned over: violence, drug abuse, cultural decay, poor education, a lack of border security, social security, poverty, threats of terrorism, and the list goes on and on. For us to spend our time and energy worrying about controversial television advertisements is a very misguided effort. Free speech is what we are guaranteed, and just like everything else in this life, it carries pros and cons. What we should be grateful for is that fact that we live in a nation where we have an agency, such as the F.C.C., to look out for us, especially our children. What is allowed to air on television is simply a reflection of what society deems to be acceptable—it's a sign of the times. It's what you and I, our families, our neighborhoods, our communities, and our cities deem acceptable. Today is a gloomy time in our nation's culture. An increasing number of children and adults fail to learn of their country's heritage and history and have lost almost all interest in the fine arts. Rap music, gore-filled movies and pornography run rampant in today's society; these are real problems and their manifestations can be seen on the daily news. Whether [it's] gang-related violence, drug dealing or rape, these cultural malignancies are tearing away at our nation.

Change starts in the home; when we begin to hold ourselves to higher standards, the second-rate music and movies will begin to disappear and our culture will once again rise to higher levels. This is not likely in the foreseeable future, though, and until then, just like a wise man once said, "we've got bigger fish to fry," than to lose sleep or waste energy even thinking about controversial television advertisements. This is no far-fetched possibility; one of the great things about the United States is that the people truly do have the power to make change. When it comes to the media, we can make or break them. The high-paid media moguls decide who's going to be rich and famous, but it's us—the people—who have the final say. If we make our voices heard, we can make real change here at home, and maybe once again enjoy the decency that our forefathers once knew.

| "Avoiding objectionable material has be-
come more difficult. . . . And one of the
more toxic areas is now the ads."

Television Ads Are Becoming More Indecent

Linda Chavez

Linda Chavez is a conservative columnist, radio host, political analyst, and chairwoman of the Center for Equal Opportunity. In the following viewpoint, she argues that a number of television ads are indecent and not family friendly. Chavez singles out ads for sex-enhancing drugs, jeans, and liquor to be especially offensive.

As you read, consider the following questions:

1. What television ads astonished Chavez when she saw them during the 2007 National League Championship Series?

2. According to the author, which television ad was the worst offender?

3. How does Chavez feel about the program guides that list channel offerings?

A m I imagining it or is television becoming even more family unfriendly? For years now, primetime television fare has offered a steady diet of comedies that depend on sexual innuendo and situations for laughs, crime dramas that make the world seem like it's filled with sadistic predators and perverts, often within our own homes, and cable "news" programs that spend as much time dissecting the bizarre antics of this week's celebrity bad girl (or boy) as they do covering real news.

But avoiding objectionable material has become more difficult, despite V-chips, which allow parents to control access to certain programs. And one of the more toxic areas is now the ads.

Sex in Television Ads

Not only do commercials try to use sex to sell everything from automobiles to soap, it seems half the ads on TV now are marketing sex itself in the form of sex-enhancing drugs. And there's no avoiding the ads, no matter how careful you are with selecting your programming.

You can block, *Desperate Housewives* or *Sex and the City* reruns, but what do you do about the ads in family programs—like Major League Baseball? I was astonished at what aired between innings of the fourth game in the National League Championship Series [NLCS] between the Colorado Rockies and the Arizona Diamondbacks, for example. The usual impotence drugs led the pack, as they do for most sports programming. You wonder how many kids out there turn to Dad to explain what "ED" [erectile dysfunction] stands for.

Then there were the liquor ads, and since the game aired on cable, these were for hard liquor, not just the usual beer commercials. No matter what messages the advertisers tack on to "drink responsibly," pushing alcohol consumption to young audiences is destructive.

But the worst offender during the NLCS was by far Levi's. Remember when the company used to sell its blue jeans with rugged cowboys outfitted in its signature 501 style denims? Now the emphasis isn't how sturdy the pants are but how quickly randy couples can get out of them. The NLCS Levi's ad featured a series of young couples, some appearing to be teenagers, ripping off their shirts as they moved toward each other to reveal yet another hot guy or gal underneath. That is until the last couple embrace, bare-torsoed and wearing only their Levi's.

Objectionable Ads for Kids and Adults

And it's not just sex, drugs and alcohol that offend decency. Many of the ads are downright horrifying for adults, much less kids. Since it's Halloween season, there's the usual Holly-wood release of the latest slasher film ad to frighten all ages, plus the many gruesome images used to advertise network shows like *Bones*, the various *CSI* and *Law and Order* incarnations, *Close to Home*, or others.

The networks plug their own shows relentlessly, as do the supposedly advertising-free premium channels. And if you happen to subscribe to channels like HBO because you're a fan of some particular series (in my case, *The Wire*, which may be the best drama ever produced for television), you can be watching something unobjectionable only to have soft-core porn flash on screen in the form of a promotion for another of the network's shows.

Even the program guides that list channel offerings can be a challenge. You may block offensive programs or channels, but just perusing the on-screen guide looking for something decent to watch can be a minefield. Recently, the PG animated movie *Happy Feet* aired right before *Cathouse*, which the guide helpfully describes as a documentary on "the Moonlite Bunny Ranch . . . a legal brothel in Nevada." And if you're looking for entertainment after 10 p.m., you'll find listings for shows like *Real Sex*, *Sin City Diaries*, or the latest HBO affront, *Katie Morgan on Sex Toys*.

You don't have to be a child, or even have children in your home, to find this intrusion of Hollywood values into your living room troublesome. But unless you're willing to throw out your set altogether, there doesn't seem [to be] much you can do about it.

> *"Should [an advocacy ad] be banned? Frankly, my first inclination is to say no."*

Advocacy Ads Should Be Allowed

Tracy Clark-Flory

Tracy Clark-Flory is a staff writer for Salon.com. In the following viewpoint, she states that although she finds certain advocacy ads troublesome and verging on propaganda, she feels that they should be allowed on free-speech grounds. Clark-Flory argues that television networks must be more consistent about what kind of commercials they air.

As you read, consider the following questions:

1. According to Clark-Flory, what is the Tim Tebow ad?

2. How much did Focus on the Family spend to air the Tebow ad during the Super Bowl, according to the author?

3. According to Clark-Flory, has CBS turned down Super Bowl ads with ideological bents before the Tebow ad?

The Super Bowl XLIV is still 12 days away [February 7, 2010], but a pre-game showdown has already begun between pro- and anti-choice activists. Focus on the Family, that paragon of "righteous" bigotry, has landed a coveted 30-second TV spot during the game that is expected to deliver an anti-abortion message, and the Women's Media Center, with the support of several reproductive rights organizations, has kicked off a campaign for CBS to ban the ad.

Here's what we know so far about the ad: It features star college quarterback Tim Tebow and his mother, Pam, sharing "a personal story centered on the theme of 'Celebrate Family, Celebrate Life,'" according to a Focus on the Family press release. It's safe to assume the spot will tell the story of how Tebow's mom fell ill during her pregnancy but refused doctors' advice that she have an abortion for her own safety. Luckily enough, she gave birth to a healthy baby boy and future Heisman Trophy–winner. Tebow only confirmed suspicions that the ad takes this tack when the controversy was raised at a recent press conference: "I've always been very convicted of it"—presumably his antiabortion view—"because that's the reason I'm here, because my mom was a very courageous woman."

Should Tebow Ad Be Banned?

Assuming this is an explicitly antiabortion advertisement, should it be banned? Frankly, my first inclination is to say no. After all, I'm a big believer in free speech, and if Focus on the Family wants to throw down anywhere from $2.5 million to $2.8 million on a Super Bowl spot, so be it. Only, while I'm no fan of censorship, I *am* a fan of consistency, and in the past CBS has banned Super Bowl ads with ideological bents. In 2004, the network turned away a United Church of Christ advertisement welcoming gay parishioners and explained that it had "a longstanding policy of not accepting advocacy adver-

USA Residents Speak Out on Advocacy Ads

In the past, television networks have been reluctant to air commercials during the Super Bowl which take a position on policy issues such as abortion, gay rights, animal rights, and smoking. Overall, do you think it is appropriate or not appropriate for so-called advocacy ads to be allowed to air during the Super Bowl?

	Appropriate Row %	Not Appropriate Row %	Unsure Row %
USA Residents	44%	49%	7%
Registered Voters	45%	49%	7%
Party ID			
Democrat	42%	51%	7%
Republican	48%	45%	7%
Independent	46%	49%	5%
Ideology			
Liberal	44%	50%	6%
Moderate	43%	52%	5%
Conservative	49%	44%	7%
Region			
Northeast	56%	40%	4%
Midwest	43%	51%	6%
South	37%	53%	9%
West	46%	47%	7%
Household income			
Less than $50,000	41%	50%	9%
$50,000 or more	48%	47%	5%
Education			
Not college graduate	42%	51%	7%
College graduate	47%	45%	7%

continued

USA Residents Speak Out on Advocacy Ads [CONTINUED]

In the past, television networks have been reluctant to air commercials during the Super Bowl which take a position on policy issues such as abortion, gay rights, animal rights, and smoking. Overall, do you think it is appropriate or not appropriate for so-called advocacy ads to be allowed to air during the Super Bowl?

	Appropriate Row %	Not Appropriate Row %	Unsure Row %
Age			
18 to 29	47%	46%	7%
30 to 44	54%	44%	2%
45 to 59	45%	48%	7%
60 or older	31%	57%	12%
Gender			
Men	47%	47%	6%
Women	41%	51%	8%

February 2010 Marist Poll National Residents "N=1,072 MOE +/−3%". Totals may not add to 100 due to rounding.

TAKEN FROM: "2/5: Advocacy Ads During Super Bowl? Public Okays Tebow Ad," Marist Poll, February 5, 2010, http://maristpoll.marist.edu.

tising." However, it seems CBS may be changing that long-standing policy. A spokesperson e-mailed the following statement:

> We have for some time moderated our approach to advocacy submissions after it became apparent that our stance did not reflect public sentiment or industry norms on the issue. In fact, most media outlets have accepted advocacy ads for some time.

Just last year, however, NBC rejected a spot from CatholicVote.org, which begged us to imagine if President Barack Obama's mother had aborted him simply because he would be raised in "a broken home," "abandoned by his father" and raised by a single mother. (By the way, there is no evidence that Obama's mother ever considered aborting him—but, pshh, *facts*.) No matter the network, the Super Bowl has a long record of rejecting advocacy ads, and for good reason: On the biggest sporting night of the year, people want their Doritos, Bud Light and Pepsi commercials, not propaganda.

Controversy over the Ad

A Focus on the Family spokesperson told the *Washington Post* that the ad isn't overtly political, but a petition by the Women's Media Center argues otherwise: "By offering one of the most coveted advertising spots of the year to an anti-equality, anti-choice, homophobic organization, CBS is aligning itself with a political stance that will damage its reputation, alienate viewers, and discourage consumers from supporting its shows and advertisers." There is no denying the organization's founder, James Dobson, is about as polarizing a political figure as they come.

Setting aside CBS' inconsistency and the larger debate about policing Super Bowl ads, we're left with Tebow's story. It's a heartwarming one—his mother wanted him, she risked her life for him and both survived. No part of me wants to prevent women from hearing that story; being pro-choice means fully educating women about the potential outcomes of their decision—including, yes, the slim possibility that against doctors' best predictions a woman and her baby survive a life-threatening pregnancy. But that isn't the whole story, and in Focus on the Family's hands it will likely be used to manipulate, not to educate; the organization isn't just antiabortion but anti-*choice*, after all. Here's hoping against all reason that the ad doesn't present the exception to the rule (e.g., Barack Obama, a miracle birth) as the rule by which women should—no, must—live by.

| *"The networks in fact have no 'guideline' for advocacy ads, they just have biases."*

Networks Should Have Consistent Standards for Airing Advocacy Ads

Jeffrey Lord

Jeffrey Lord is a former White House political director from the Ronald Reagan administration and an author. In the following viewpoint, he maintains that CBS showed its biases by airing the controversial antiabortion Tim Tebow ad after it had rejected other advocacy ads in the past. Lord also contends that CBS did it for the money.

As you read, consider the following questions:

1. According to the author, what was the controversial United Church of Christ ad that was rejected by CBS in 2004?

2. How did the Gallup poll on political affiliation influence CBS executives, according to Lord?

3. What does the author say about Reverend Guess's statement on CBS?

Jeffrey Lord, "CBS Double Standard: Network and Church Battle over Ads," *American Spectator*, February 2, 2010. Copyright © 2010 by American Spectator. Reproduced by permission.

Forget the Colts and the Saints.

The real struggle this Super Bowl season is between The Network and The Church.

This year's [2010's] brawl involves a fight between CBS and the United Church of Christ, only by extension featuring [2007] Heisman Trophy winner Tim Tebow and his mom Pam. Pam, as all of America is learning, was pregnant with her fifth child and advised to have an abortion. She refused—giving birth to a man who went on to win one of college football's most prestigious awards, becoming in the process, in the eyes of many, a genuine celebration of life. . . .

But there is another problem here. It seems the ad, sponsored by Dr. James Dobson's Focus on the Family, was accepted by CBS—when CBS, not all that long ago, rejected a fairly innocuous ad from the United Church of Christ [UCC] proclaiming the denomination's inclusivity when it comes to gays.

The fair and balanced people at Fox ran it, many others as well, but not CBS (or even NBC!)

As always, a disclaimer that I serve as both the president of my local UCC church and a board member of the Penn Central Conference—and do not speak for either in this space.

CBS Has No Credibility on This Issue

It may startle the liberal national hierarchy of my denomination to know I believe the UCC has a case. A very good case.

Yes, it must be acknowledged that CBS gets to set its standards for accepting advertising. That is its right. And at a time when Americans feel a move is on to strip them of their rights, most prominently by taking away control of their health care, a TV network's right to choose its advertisers is a freedom that should be noted. But having a right—and this particular right is a right tempered by the fact of access to airwaves owned by the public—is a very different thing from having credibility.

Plainly put, CBS has no credibility on this.

[The ad CBS rejected in 2004 is] a very vanilla take on what the liberals running the church see as the denomination's inclusiveness. Nothing over the top, nothing offensive. Just the straight (so to speak) message that the UCC is inclusive, that, in the words of the UCC, "all people, including gay and lesbian people, should be welcome in the church." It takes no stand on same-sex marriage (although the national church leadership famously did so—in favor—in 2005, causing an internal firestorm, but that's another story.). The ad, in other words, is hardly earthshaking.

Yet for some reason, CBS put this benign ad (not submitted for a Super Bowl time period) in the same category as those infamous banned Super Bowl ads of years past. Remember those?

Other Controversial Super Bowl Ads

Let's see. There was the Ashley Madison [online dating service] ad that was promoting extra-marital affairs with the tag line "Who are you doing after the game?" The ad from the People for the Ethical Treatment of Animals (PETA) depicting lingerie-clad women, none of them ugly, getting . . . ahhhh . . . "intimate" with vegetables. Remember the 2005 ad from GoDaddy.com that mocked the Janet Jackson wardrobe malfunction episode [during the halftime show of 2004's Super Bowl, Jackson's breast was briefly exposed] with a busty woman testifying before Congress as her top keeps sliding off? Or the cold remedy ad showing a bare-chested, towel-wrapped Mickey Rooney (he's not a kid anymore) in a sauna? That gem was pulled because the towel dropped briefly (!) exposing America to the long-ago child star's, um, then almost 90-year-old butt. Yikes. Mr. Rooney turned 90 recently. God bless him

Super Bowl's Attraction: The Game or the Ads?

Do you watch the Super Bowl:

	More for the Game Row %	More for the Commercials Row %
Residents planning to watch the Super Bowl	78%	22%
Region		
Northeast	83%	17%
Midwest	71%	29%
South	77%	23%
West	82%	18%
Household income		
Less than $50,000	79%	21%
$50,000 or more	79%	21%
Age		
Under 45	76%	24%
45 or older	79%	21%
Gender		
Men	86%	14%
Women	68%	32%

"N=730 MOE +/−4%". Numbers may not add to 100 due to rounding.

TAKEN FROM: "2/5: Advocacy Ads During Super Bowl? Public Okays Tebow Ad," Marist Poll, February 5, 2010. http://maristpoll.marist.edu.

. . . here's to keeping his pants on during the Super Bowl. Then there was the Snickers ad from 2007, which showed two guys working on a car when one suddenly stops and pulls out a Snicker bar. The other starts chomping on the free end, leading to an accidental kiss and the declaration they needed to go do something "manly." Gay groups got that one banned. In 2008, it was sexy models driving up in cars to some fictional big media event with live beavers in their laps (meant to be a visual joke on celebs Britney Spears and Lindsay Lohan, who at the time were in the tabloids for emerging from cars with, quite visibly to the paparazzi, no underwear) only to be followed by race car driver Danica Patrick, who proclaimed this not necessary and began unzipping her sporty GoDaddy.com top for photographers.

So. The United Church of Christ ad is in this category? Really? It's ridiculous on its face.

Show Me the Money

CBS, in accepting the Tebow ad because it apparently needs the bucks, has quite vividly exposed what many people on all sides of the political spectrum have long suspected: that the networks in fact have no "guideline" for advocacy ads, they just have biases. Making money—or not losing money—is at the top of that list. Understandably, that may be the only thing on their list, which under most circumstances is a good thing because making money provides exactly what Americans say they want most—jobs. And whatever else one can say about the people working at CBS, it's good news they have jobs.

Yet clearly, from a financial standpoint, CBS reads the polls. As a matter of fact, CBS as a news organization also reports the polls, as it did when it reported a January 7, 2010 Gallup Poll that says 40% of Americans identify themselves as conservatives, 36% as moderates and only a meager 20% identify as liberals. It takes very little in the way of imagination to conclude that CBS executives, hard pressed financially, took one look at the CBS News reporting here and quickly realized a pro-life ad from a conservative organization that featured a Heisman Trophy winner and his pro-life mom who took pro-choicers at their word and celebrates her choice was itself a sure ratings winner during the Super Bowl.

If the Polls Were Reversed

What troubles is that it takes even less imagination to realize that if those poll numbers were exactly reversed, with 40% of Americans calling themselves liberals to only a 20% score for conservatives—and Indianapolis Colts quarterback Peyton Manning were both gay and living with a guy he said he wanted to marry—the UCC would have had itself a network begging to run their ad and the Tim Tebow ad would be out in the cold with the ads featuring beavers, come-ons, and Mickey Rooney's bare butt.

Says the UCC's spokesman, our old sparring partner the Rev. J. Bennett Guess:

> While CBS is reportedly saying that a bad economy now ne-
> cessitates changes in its policy on so-called advocacy ads,
> this decision only underscores the arbitrary way the net-
> works approach these decisions and the result is a woeful
> lack of religious diversity in our nation's media.

Rev. Guess has it exactly right here. CBS is playing a game, it is being arbitrary—and not just with the UCC but with Focus on the Family and all the rest of us. Is the Tebow ad a good idea? Of course. The fact that a pro-life ad features such a compelling story is terrific. Good for Dr. Dobson for illustrating an important point in the culture wars.

Free Speech Goes Both Ways

But the real point here, once again, is decidedly not about abortion or gay rights or the substance of any other issue. It has nothing to do with Dr. Dobson or the UCC. It is, in fact, about the right of free expression. Not agreement with this, that, or the other idea expressed—but the right to free expression itself. Which is to say in this case, free speech. The right to speak for those who are strongly pro-life—and for those who do not agree. The right to speak for those who have a pro-same-sex marriage stance—and for those who do not agree. The right to free speech is not the same as agreement. But if we're waiting for that day when 100% of the American people will agree on 100% of the issues out there—it will be a long, very silent wait. I'm on Tim Tebow's side. I believe in traditional marriage. But never for a moment should those who believe otherwise be shut out of the debate.

UCC Must Be Consistent Too

When it comes to the right to free speech, the national UCC has itself not done well recently. Its efforts to censor or intimidate the free speech of [conservative] commentators Rush Limbaugh, Glenn Beck, Lou Dobbs and Bill O'Reilly with its "So We Might See" campaign ... [have been reported in detail].

The National Organization for Women, NARAL [Pro-Choice America], and the Women's Media Center have hopped on the censorship train this time, shockingly—and correctly—being called to account by no less than the *New York Times* editorial page. Calling these groups "would-be censors" the *Times* states what should be obvious:

> Instead of trying to silence an opponent, advocates for allowing women to make their own decisions about whether to have a child should be using the Super Bowl spotlight to convey what their movement is all about: protecting the right of women like Pam Tebow to make their private reproductive choices.

Exactly.

To hold to the same kind of double standard on speech as CBS is the only thing that weakens the UCC's case here. This continues to be an unnecessary struggle for the church hierarchy at the national level, as witness this from the Reverend Guess, also taken from his statement on CBS:

> The issue for all of us should be why one religious viewpoint is continually accommodated by the TV networks

when there is a common misunderstanding in this country that all religious people hold a monolithic view on certain issues, such as reproductive choice, such as homosexuality, and this is not the case.

Reverend Guess is simultaneously correct if disingenuous. Yes, there may be a "common misunderstanding" that assumes a religious monolith out there across the land, with difficulty perceiving the differences between faiths. Yet Rev. Guess himself is trying to imply something here that is also just not true. The fact is that the United Church of Christ itself does "not hold a monolithic view on certain issues, such as reproductive choice, such as homosexuality . . ."

Representing Different Opinions

To indicate otherwise, as Rev. Guess is trying to do here, simply doesn't represent the facts on the ground. Side-by-side in the UCC pews sit members who are pro-choice and pro-life, pro-same-sex marriage and pro-traditional marriage. We have [President Barack] Obama supporters and [former president George W.] Bush voters, liberals and conservatives, moderates and those who simply don't care about politics much at all. There are those who favor ObamaCare [Obama's health-care reform package] and those who are strongly opposed, those who love Rush [Limbaugh] and those who can't abide him. Which is to say, they are the children of God exercising precisely the human qualities of independence of thought and free speech that, to borrow a phrase from the Declaration of Independence, has been "endowed by their Creator." And by the way, the famous lead signature on the Declaration belongs to one of the more notable of lay leaders in the UCC's history—John Hancock.

Independence of thought and free speech are in fact highly valued traditions within the UCC, springing precisely from the history that had the church's earliest leaders sent to the gallows for dissent.

There are no gallows for dissent in America today, in considerable part thanks to the earliest members of this church like Hancock and his fellow UCC layman John Adams, who helped frame the basic documents that protect our human rights. But there is a disturbing tendency, ironically, that has surfaced in the UCC leadership that is unwelcoming to dissent, that tries to give the impression they speak for all members on any manner of issues like abortion when in fact they can speak for none.

We Can't Ignore Differing Opinions

It is the same reasoning that is, in addition to finances, surely at the core of the CBS decision not to show the UCC ad. CBS is manifestly uncomfortable showing even the mildest of ads that implies tolerance for gays in the same fashion that Rev. Guess leads people to believe the UCC is manifestly uncomfortable admitting its ranks are filled with pro-lifers. The same dynamic, the same impulse—to repress the uncomfortable Other and simply deny its existence—is ironically present in the hierarchies of both network and church. This hyper-political correctness is seen repeatedly all over America in incidents as varied as denying Rush Limbaugh a chance to buy an ownership role of an NFL [National Football League] team, (grossly slandering him with made-up comments that he never uttered), the recent banning of Webster's dictionary from the Menifee, California school district because it contained offensive words and for that matter the banning of all manner of other books ranging from the *Harry Potter* series to John Steinbeck's *Of Mice and Men* and Mark Twain's *Huckleberry Finn*.

The United Church of Christ should never be on the side of book banners and burners, of those who wish to hush-Rush or Drop Dobbs. All too easily the tables can be turned, which is exactly the effect of the CBS decision to ban the UCC ad.

CBS Must Set Standards

CBS should have one crystal clear standard for those advocacy groups—be it Dr. Dobson's Focus on the Family or the United Church of Christ—who wish to pony up the bucks to advertise on national television.

At the moment, what CBS has is a standard—a double standard. It might begin to make amends by finally running that UCC ad.

During the Super Bowl.

> *"It's truly amazing that hundreds of millions of dollars each year is spent on products sold through infomercials."*

Infomercials Are an Effective Way of Advertising

Matthew Maudlin

Matthew Maudlin works for Three Hats Marketing, a marketing company based in Indianapolis, Indiana. In the following viewpoint, he argues for infomercials as a particularly effective way to sell products and outlines the characteristics of a successful infomercial.

As you read, consider the following questions:

1. What does Maudlin believe is the first step to creating a great infomercial?

2. How does the seller create need, according to the author?

3. According to Maudlin, when does an infomercial *not* make you buy?

Have you ever bought something on an infomercial? Chances are you have. It's truly amazing that hundreds of millions of dollars each year is spent on products sold through infomercials. It is big business.

But did you ever stop to think how in 28 minutes and 30 seconds they can take you from not knowing of their product to picking up the phone and placing an order? (That's the part that is truly amazing.)

So how do they do it? How can I go from Sham What(?) to Sham WOW [superabsorbent towel] and actually be excited to buy one in such short time? It's all about mastering the customer buying process—and there is no better example of it than an infomercial.

Here is the steps of the customer buying process and thus the steps an infomercial takes you through.

1. *Create Awareness*. First all infomercials must introduce you to their product. They make no assumption that you have ever heard of the product before. They outline all the features of the product in high detail showing you the ins and outs of everything about it.

2. *Create Need*. Next after you are aware of the features of their product, they walk you through all the benefits. How their product will save you time, or money, or hassle, or all three. Typically they solve a problem you didn't realize you had until they point it out to you—and all that creates need.

3. *Create Urgency*. Next, infomercials are masters at creating urgency. Have you ever seen an infomercial that had a timer going in the corner of the screen? "Call in the next 30 minutes and pay just 3 payments instead of 4!" They force you to believe that now's the time to act on this need.

The Success of Infomercials

Last year [2008] more than 30% of Americans ordered a product from a television infomercial.

Seth Brown, USA Today, April 13, 2009.

4. *Evaluate Choices.* Once the viewer actually needs a product like this and is looking to buy one, they typically compare themselves to other options. Other products can't possibly do it better, or faster than their product. Comparing other options that a buyer may be considering and showing what is better about their product removes these other options from consideration

5. *Resolve Final Risk.* Lastly, there is always no risk. "If you are not 100% satisfied, just return it for a full refund. What do you have to lose?" They know if you try it, there is little chance of you returning it, so "what do they have to lose" by making an offer like that?

So those are the steps of the buying process as it relates to an infomercial. Now, what can we learn from that and apply to our [own] business?

Communicate with Your Prospects in This Order

This is a great model for us to consider when we are working with prospects. Model your marketing and sales presentations after the organizational structure of the infomercial, and you might be surprised at the success you find yourself having. If nothing else, you may learn where people are getting hung up in the process and where you might need to improve your tactics. . . .

[Skipping a step] is something we try to do all the time. We present information to prospects when they are not ready to receive it. We share the price before they feel they need our product or service, so it goes on deaf ears, or the perceived value is lower than our price. Or sometimes we neglect to remove the final risk—thus putting their mind at ease with their decision and therefore never close the deal. Pay attention to the prospect's questions and hear what they really need to know from you. Don't move ahead in the process without making sure they're along with you.

Moving Buyers to the Next Step

When does an infomercial *not* make you buy? When their tactics don't move to the next step in the process. Maybe they didn't create the need or the urgency for you or remove the risk for you. Regardless, you didn't move yourself through the process—and therefore they didn't get a sale. Now of course, they can't stop a 30 minute program just for you—they have to keep going. But when you are working with your prospects, make sure they are moving along with you in the process. If not, go back to where you left them off. Give these thoughts some consideration and if they make sense, apply them to your next presentation. If you need assistance in taking your presentations to the next level, give us a call. I promise it won't be a waste of your time—you have our 100% money back guarantee.

| *"Everything being sold through infomercials is completely ridiculous and unnecessary!"*

Infomercials Are Useless and Prey on the Vulnerable

John Jacobs

John Jacobs is a columnist for the Minaret, *the University of Tampa's student-run newspaper. In the following viewpoint, he contends that infomercials prey on bored viewers and offer solutions to problems that do not exist. Jacobs argues that although infomercials can be entertaining, they pertain to problems most viewers cannot really relate to.*

As you read, consider the following questions:

1. According to the author, when do infomercials usually air?

2. According to Jacobs, how do infomercials usually start?

3. How do infomercials usually end, according to the author?

This week [November 2009] I wanted to talk about info-mercials in honor of one of my heroes who recently passed away, [infomercial host] Billy Mays (because just like his products, he was only available for a limited time).

Infomercials usually pop up when watching any main TV stations like Fox, NBC or CBS around 2 a.m. And they catch you off guard, too; you don't question it until it seems extra long and you start to think to yourself, "Wait, has this commercial been on for 12 minutes now?"

What Infomercials Are

All these infomercials usually start the same way, a voice will come on and say something like, "Does this happen to you daily?" Then it'll cut to a clip in black and white of a woman bending over to pick something up and immediately jerks back to grab her back in pain while shaking her head and staring at the camera as if to say, "If only there were a better way!"

The voice comes back—"Well those days are over because the Mighty Claw is here!"—and the pitch begins. A man will walk into the shot (usually in a living room or kitchen) and start telling you random facts about some "horrible" situation people have to go through every day. "Did you know the average person in America bends over to pick things up [up] to seven times a day? And did you know every time you bend over you cause stress in your back, which could lead to arthritis and scoliosis? Well now those problems can finally be solved with the Mighty Claw!" (Thank God! I smell a Nobel Peace Prize.)

Showcasing the Product

A rundown of what the product is made of and examples of what it can do then follow.

"The Mighty Claw is made up of a retracting three piece set of Japanese titanium rods, which extend on command, equipped with a rubber handle with a graphite finish which homes the easy-access hand trigger giving you control of the stainless steel claws on the end."

He then walks over to an area with random items on the floor. "For example, look at that newspaper on the floor! If I didn't have the Mighty Claw, who knows how long or how many tries it would take me to bend over and pick it up? But now with the lightweight six pounds Mighty Claw, bending over becomes a thing of the past!" (Finally! I was so tired of having to use my body to do things!)

Then finally after this whole presentation (keep in mind showing off the product and informing you on it does take around 30 minutes), we come to the price of this amazing product. They start by comparing their price to similar products, which makes you think, "Why would more than one of these exist anyway?" The man will say something like, "Competitors may charge you up to $600 for a similar product! But with this special TV offer, you can get the mighty claw for 69 easy payments of $3.99! However, if you order within the next full moon, we'll throw in a second mighty claw absolutely free!"

Detailing the Savings

Then to wrap everything up and to give you one last reason in case you still have any doubts, they give you an estimation of how much money you'll save by buying this product. "When you buy the Mighty Claw you'll potentially save at least $10,000 on back surgery and prescription pain killers for the rest of your life! Can you really afford to miss out on this deal?"

First off, if you need a payment plan to buy something off an infomercial, you probably have bigger problems than whatever it is the product can "fix." Also, what part of these numerous payments is "easy?" If anything, wouldn't spreading the payments out over time instead of just paying all at once be much more inconvenient? I don't want to still be paying for my Slap Chop [food chopper sold by infomercial] two years after it breaks.

Second, I don't like when they need to threaten me into buying the product with random statistics and "potential savings." The arguments are usually so random and unrelated to the product in any way, it really has nothing to do with anything. "Did you know around 151,000 people die every day? (Actual fact) Well, if you buy Axe Body Spray, you might not die today!" And third, everything being sold through infomercials is completely ridiculous and unnecessary!

Unnecessary Products

Can anybody really say the Snuggie was a good idea? I'm pretty sure this was invented when someone woke up extremely hung over one day, put a robe on backwards, walked downstairs and when he was asked about what he was wearing, he was too stubborn to admit he'd made a mistake, and that's how the Snuggie came to be. I guarantee if your parents showed up to your high school football game wearing Snuggies like in the commercials, you would be too ashamed to admit you were their child. (But I'm guessing if you own a Snuggie you're not planning on going out in public any time soon.)

As entertaining as these infomercials are, it's sad that people can actually relate to the problems shown in these commercials. I think if I'm sitting with a friend watching an infomercial, and he says to me, "Dude, finally! I am always struggling to make waffles in the microwave!" we probably wouldn't be friends for much longer.

So next time you're watching TV, and it cuts to a black and white clip of a woman fumbling to fill her oven with dirty dishes while she gets handed divorce papers from a lawyer, get excited to finally learn how to overcome some annoying daily chores.

"[The DVR] threatens both networks and advertisers."

DVRs Threaten Television Advertising

BusinessWeek

BusinessWeek *is a weekly business magazine published by Bloomberg. In the following viewpoint,* BusinessWeek *reports that digital video recorders (DVRs) are becoming a real threat to traditional television advertising, because DVRs allow viewers to skip television commercials.*

As you read, consider the following questions:

1. How many American homes were estimated to use DVRs by the end of 2007, according to researcher In-Stat, as cited by *BusinessWeek*?

2. According to Nielsen Media Research, as cited by the author, what percentage of US households had DVRs in 2006?

3. According to In-Stat, as cited by *BusinessWeek* in a survey of 406 DVR owners, what percentage report using the skip function regularly?

Zapping commercials seemed like a threat the networks could afford to deal with later. Well, later is here. Since December [2005] ratings agency Nielsen Media Research Inc. has been revising its measurements to include how many folks TiVo, or record, shows to be watched later—with the option of skipping the ads. Nielsen now has the numbers to provide a meaningful picture of what's going on out there. And it's sure to make network brass squirm.

Based on *BusinessWeek*'s analysis of the Nielsen numbers, when *American Idol* judge Simon Cowell eviscerated crooner Ace Young on Apr. 18, [2006,] some 1 million homes caught the action an hour or more later on their digital video-recorders (DVRs). Of those viewers, perhaps 800,000 fast-forwarded past the commercials.

DVRs aren't yet ubiquitous in America. Fewer than 5% of *Idol*'s 28.5 million viewers TiVoed the Apr. 18 show, and a relatively tiny half-million or so people did the same for recent episodes of CBS's *Without a Trace* and *CSI: New York*. But with the cable guys pushing DVR technology hard, 20% of U.S. viewers could be in a position to zap ads by the end of [2007], according to researcher In-Stat.

Pam McNeely, group media director at Dailey & Associates Advertising, figures the number could go to 40%. "You tell that to clients," she says, "and they say, 'Oh, my God! I'm cutting TV spending.'"

You can bet the DVR will be a divisive issue as network executives and advertisers gather in New York this month [May 2006] for the annual "upfront" scrum, when most of the haggling over ad rates happens. Some big ad agencies say they intend to pay only for "live" viewing, such as the 10.6 million homes that tuned in recently for ABC's *Grey's Anatomy*.

Mike Shaw, ABC's sales president, publicly blasted the ad industry's position as "unfair and unjust" and intimated he wouldn't negotiate with those who won't pay for more than live viewers. He and his counterparts at the other networks ar-

How Do You Rate the Impact in the Next 3 Years on the Effectiveness of TV Advertising of...

Respondents: Advertisers and Advertising Agencies

	Very negative	Somewhat negative	No impact	Somewhat positive	Very positive	Do Not Know	Average Score
The trend to watch TV programs on newer platforms (internet, mobile, etc.)	7%	41%	7%	31%	11%	3%	0.0
The increase in the number of TV channels (channel proliferation)	8%	31%	26%	28%	4%	3%	−0.1
The increase in access to and use of video-on-demand	7%	50%	16%	16%	8%	3%	−0.3
The decrease in TV consumption from increased use of newer entertainment formats (games, internet)	10%	48%	23%	12%	4%	3%	−0.5
The increase in the number and use of DVRs	18%	62%	5%	9%	2%	3%	−0.9

Very negative ■ Somewhat negative ■ No impact ■ Somewhat positive ■ Very positive

Number of observations: Advertisers: 72, Advertising Agencies: 112

TAKEN FROM: "Advertising in the DVR Age," DVR Research Institute, 2010.

gue that DVR households are watching more shows now that they can record programs to watch later. And CBS, ABC, NBC, and Fox participated in a study that found DVR owners are more likely to pay attention to ads than viewers who may leave or zone out during the commercial breaks. The upshot: Network executives want their rates based on the total number of viewers, including those who see a show later.

Hustling to Adapt

The networks will find it harder to defend their position as Nielsen gets better at tracking DVR use. So far the agency gathers that metric in only 5% of the 12,000 homes in its national sample. But Nielsen says about 11% of U.S. households have DVRs [in 2006]. That means the 593,000 homes Nielsen says recorded *American Idol* may be closer to 1.2 million. And while it's hard to put a precise number on ad skipping, the practice seems common. In a survey of 406 DVR owners, says senior In-Stat analyst Mike Paxton, 87% said they used the skip function frequently.

For all their combativeness, the networks and advertisers are hustling to adapt. A new Ford Motor spot on *American Idol* features the cut-down lineup of contestants and is shot to look like part of the show, a ploy to prevent viewers from zapping the ad. And advertisers already are negotiating for perks, including first placement in each string of commercials, so viewers will see some of their ad before they manage to grab the remote, says Garth Ancier, outgoing chairman of The WB Network: "That's all about the DVR."

With fewer than 3% of ads being zapped, the TV advertising model is far from dead. But with the Age of the DVR upon us, it's in serious need of corrective surgery. "The two sides have to talk now, because [the DVR] threatens both networks and advertisers if they don't," says Brad Adgate, research vice-president at ad consultant Horizon Media Inc. There's no zapping past that grim reality.

| "Advertisers are now empowered with capabilities to fully leverage DVR technology and connect with their desired consumers."

DVRs Benefit Television Advertising

PR Newswire

PR Newswire is a leading global vendor in information and news distribution services for professional communicators. In the following viewpoint, the author contends that DVRs (digital video recorders) will not devastate television advertisers. TiVo has provided advertisers with the ability to understand DVR technology and the impact it has on product sales and advertising. This resource not only allows marketers to understand viewers' habits, but provides a way for media testing and advertising to advance in a DVR world.

As you read, consider the following questions:

1. What does the IRI TiVo Consumer Pulse provide advertisers, according to PR Newswire?

2. What does the IRI BehaviorScan allow advertisers and brand marketers to do, in the author's opinion?

PR Newswire, "TiVo Information Resources Inc. Launch Groundbreaking TV Advertising Research Services," September 20, 2006. Reproduced by permission.

3. According to Sunil Garga, as quoted by PR Newswire, how does the combination of IRI TiVo Consumer Pulse and BehaviorScan information benefit advertisers?

TiVo Inc. and Information Resources, Inc. (IRI), today [September 20, 2006,] launched the IRI TiVo Consumer Insights Suite(TM), comprised of two new services, providing advertisers and brand marketers with the ability to fully understand the impact digital video recorder (DVR) technology has on consumer viewing patterns and subsequent product sales, as well as the ability to quantify the effectiveness of specific advertising campaigns and brand recognition programs in TiVo(R) DVR households.

Additionally, TiVo, the creator of and leader in advertising solutions and television services for DVRs, and IRI, the world's leading provider of enterprise market information solutions and services for the consumer packaged goods (CPG), retail, and healthcare industries, are expanding their existing relationship. Utilizing second-by-second analysis and tracking it to actual consumer purchasing decisions, the expanded relationship provides first-of-its-kind viewer and consumer insights from a new national DVR research panel combined with new media and message testing capabilities to fully understand and better leverage the evening impact of DVRs.

"TiVo continues to take innovative steps to help advertisers analyze and measure the effectiveness of their campaigns by combining unrivaled, second-by-second viewer data with verified consumer purchase decisions," said TiVo Chief Executive Officer Tom Rogers.

Todd Juenger, Vice President & General Manager, TiVo Audience Research & Measurement added, "The IRI TiVo Consumer Insights Suite provides rich, new consumer insights about TiVo usage and sales impact along with a world-class testing capability to fully understand how advertising . . . is

Summary of Key Findings—All Four Surveyed Markets

Question	U.K.	U.S.	Italy	Australia
Average number of hours of TV watched per day (live & recorded)	3.7	4.7	4.1	3.8
Agree that since getting a DVR they are more likely to find something to watch, when they want to watch	77%	83%	75%	72%
Those with partners who found that having a DVR has improved their relationship	62%	79%	78%	78%
Those with families who found that having a DVR has improved family life	64%	81%	82%	76%
Those with one DVR who would like to get a second	30%	52%	57%	49%
Ranked the DVR as the second most indispensable household technology item, after the mobile phone	78%	81%	73%	75%
Ranked the DVR as the third most indispensable household item after the washing machine and the microwave	70%	62%	59%*	67%

*ranked fourth

TAKEN FROM: "More Than 80 Percent of Americans with a DVR Can't Live Without It, According to NDS Survey," NDS, September 3, 2008. http://www.nds.com.

viewed, processed and acted upon in the real world. No other research solution available today can deliver as detailed insight and analysis as this."

Panel Delivers New Insights

The IRI TiVo Consumer Pulse(TM) solution provides advertisers with completely new TV viewer and consumers sales insights on the effect of DVR time-shifting behavior on sales through an opt-in panel of viewing participants throughout the United States. The new solution identifies sales impact for individual products and brands, delivers new insights on consumers being impacted, and provides new information on the viewing behaviors that actually drive the impact. Using a national opt-in panel of TiVo homes, generic DVR homes and non-DVR homes, IRI measures brand purchases to deliver a new understanding of brand performance in DVR households and the impact of DVRs on product launches, brand extensions, and established brands. TiVo then measures second-by-second commercial viewership in the homes with TiVo service, making it possible for brand purchase results to be traced and compared to the actual viewership of commercials.

Advancing Media Testing

Through the IRI BehaviorScan(R) DVR solution, brand marketers, advertisers, advertising agencies, media networks and cable operators will be able to test specific advertising . . . while simultaneously tracking the purchasing behavior of TiVo households and compare that with generic DVR and non-DVR households within the same market. Advertisers will benefit from the highly-controlled, split-test environment, enabling them to execute different advertising plans based on what is most actionable and relevant to their target audience. Advertisers and media buyers will also be able to experiment with media, mix, and creative strategies to prepare for a world of DVR ubiquity before it becomes a reality.

"DVR penetration continues to grow throughout the United States and advertisers need to be equipped with the most informative insights and solutions available to maximize effectiveness and ROI [return on investment] of marketing communications," said IRI President and Chief Executive Officer Scott W. Klein.

"In this innovative media landscape, advertisers must be equally innovative in understanding consumers' media habits to effectively reach their target market," said IRI President of Business and Consumer Insights Sunil Garga. "Using the unique combination of IRI TiVo Consumer Pulse Information and BehaviorScan testing capabilities with second-by-second TiVo data, advertisers are now empowered with capabilities to fully leverage DVR technology and connect with their desired consumers in the correct way."

TiVo and IRI first partnered in 2004 when IRI supplied TiVo DVRs to a subset of its BehaviorScan household panelists, providing a consortium of select major CPG companies critical data on the impact of their advertising programs.

All of the panelists who choose to participate in the program have expressly agreed to "opt-in" to allow TiVo to track their exact viewing behavior in order to form the basis for comparison.

Periodical Bibliography

The following articles have been selected to supplement the diverse views presented in this chapter.

Robin Abcarian "Tebow Ad Falls Short of the Hype," *Los Angeles Times*, February 8, 2010.

Boston Globe "Show Tebow Ad, but Be Fair," February 6, 2010.

Tracy Clark-Flory "CBS Helped with Tebow Ad," Salon.com, February 2, 2010.

Bill Coffin "But Wait . . . There's More!" *Risk Management*, June 2009.

Brooke E. Crescent "Undercover Marketing," *Journal of Law and Policy*, Fall 2005.

Marybeth Hicks "Indecent Ads Are a No-Sell," *Washington Times*, December 16, 2009.

Sally Jenkins "Tebow's Super Bowl Ad Isn't Intolerant; His Critics Are," *Washington Post*, February 2, 2010.

Patrik Jonsson "Tim Tebow Super Bowl Ad: An Astonishingly Bold Stand," *Christian Science Monitor*, January 27, 2010.

Corey Kilgannon "Step on Up, Make a Pitch to the King of Pitchmen," *New York Times*, December 16, 2009.

Troy Patterson "No Extra Charge," *Slate*, April 13, 2009. www.slate.com.

Catherine Saint Louis "A Face from an Infomercial," *New York Times*, June 4, 2009.

USA Today "'Miracle' Tim Tebow Super Bowl Ad Puts Hit on Critic," February 7, 2010.

OPPOSING
VIEWPOINTS®
SERIES

How Should Television Be Regulated?

Chapter Preface

Many American parents are concerned with the increasing amount of violence on television. For years, violence has been a staple in many prime-time shows: portrayals of murders, war scenes, assaults, car chases, and torture can be found on any given night on one or more television programs broadcast on network or cable television—and parents are alarmed that their children are seeing that violence. A 2007 study published by the Federal Communications Commission (FCC) reported that the average US household has a television set turned on an average of 8 hours and 11 minutes every single day. Much of that television watching is being done by children. In fact, by the time most kids enter first grade, they've already viewed more than three school years' worth of television programming.

Such alarming statistics on the amount of time American children spent in front of the television led the FCC to consider ways to protect them from violent TV programs. One such solution to the problem was the V-chip, a technology that allowed parents to block certain programs so that their children could not view them. It was available in televisions beginning in 1999; however, by the mid-2000s, the FCC was arguing that the V-chip had failed as an effective monitoring device because not enough parents were buying or using them. Voluntary ratings programs, which allow the networks to rate the amount and type of violence portrayed, are also regarded as a failure. The FCC maintains that networks consistently underrated the amount and severity of the violence on their programming.

After a reevaluation of policy, the 2007 FCC report "Violent Television Programming and Its Impact on Children," urged Congress to consider regulations that would restrict violent programs to late evening (after 10 PM) when most children would be in bed. This is called time channeling. The FCC also proposed a mandatory labeling system and that consumers be allowed the option to buy cable channels individually or in bundles so that they would not have to buy channels that they did not want their kids watching.

Civil libertarians and many media commentators argue that parents—not the FCC—should be the ones monitoring their children's television viewing and that parents should determine what is "excessive" violence, not some government agency.

Defining "excessive" or "unacceptable" violence has been a sticking point for the FCC for a number of years. It has proven to be a very difficult task. In the 2007 report, however, the FCC proposes that such a definition *can* be crafted—one that will hold up as constitutional in a court of law. Moreover, because the television networks have a more limited right to free speech because of their power and pervasiveness, the FCC asserts that it has the right to regulate the issue of violence on television.

Defining and regulating excessive violence grew increasingly important in light of evidence illuminating the effect of such violence on impressionable children. The 2007 FCC report refers to a range of studies that indicate a connection between violent behavior in children and violent images on television—findings supported by important groups such as the American Medical Association and the American Psychological Association. With such links established, the impetus behind protecting children from violence on television continues to gain momentum.

Regulating violence on television is one of the topics debated in this chapter, which focuses on how television should be regulated. Other issues discussed include the regulation of indecent language and the volume levels of television commercials.

> "It came down to federal intervention after Hollywood's absolute refusal to live up to its stated commitment at self-regulation."

The Government Must Regulate Indecency on Television

L. Brent Bozell III

L. Brent Bozell III is the president of the Media Research Center. In the following viewpoint, he asserts that the television networks' attempts at self-regulation have been a joke and as a result the television airwaves are rife with indecency. Bozell praises passage of the Broadcast Decency Enforcement Act, a law that increases maximum fines for indecent programming, as a step in the right direction.

As you read, consider the following questions:

1. According to the author, how much did maximum fines increase with the passage of the Broadcast Decency Enforcement Act?

L. Brent Bozell III, "Empowering the FCC," Townhall.com, June 16, 2006. Copyright © 2006 by Creators Syndicate. Reproduced by permission.

2. What was the vote for the Broadcast Decency Enforcement Act in the House of Representatives, according to Bozell?

3. Why does the author believe that the V-chip was destined to fail?

On June 15, [2006,] President [George W.] Bush held a signing ceremony at the White House for the Broadcast Decency Enforcement Act, a new law increasing the maximum fine for indecent TV programming tenfold, from $32,500 to $325,000 per violation.

The president knows the problem. The current maximum "is meaningless. It's relatively painless for them when they violate decency standards. And so the Congress decided to join the administration and do something about it. . . . The Congress got serious."

Bipartisan Agreement

It may have taken three years too many, but when Congress finally acted, it did so in an overwhelmingly bi-partisan fashion seldom seen in Washington anymore. The House bill passed by a 397 to 35 margin. The Senate version sailed through unanimously.

And why not? The public, in red and blue states alike, is fed up with the raw sexual sewage and graphic violence being poured onto the airwaves they own. A December [2005] Associated Press poll found 66 percent of those surveyed said there was too much sex on TV, and 68 percent said there was too much violence. Other polls have pegged public disgust in the 80- and 90-percent levels.

In that sense, it was a no-brainer vote, but this is Washington, D.C., where nothing is simple, and ultimately, it also took real courage. Credit should flow to the Congress and the president for risking offending a very powerful lobby in the broad-

Implement the Delay

Whether the live program is news, sports or any other form of entertainment, a simple seven-second delay for obscene surprises would put an end to the problem immediately. . . . The networks are refusing to do this with a very simple reason that they want to broadcast obscene language.

L. Brent Bozell III, Townhall.com,
December 8, 2008. http://townhall.com.

casters, who not only broadcast filthy entertainment, but also broadcast the news, which helps people decide whom to elect to the Congress and the presidency.

An Inconvenient Truth

The Congress and the president heard, and responded to the outcry. The broadcast networks have been, and continue to be, tone-deaf. How can our media elite find so much pessimism in our society about our future in Iraq, or our future planetary health, or our future economic success, and totally ignore the public's pessimism about how Hollywood—that is to say, *they*—are polluting the culture? The media barons are opposed to the public interest in a shameless, grasping, greedy way, every bit as shameless as these networks have portrayed the Big Oil barons in the last few months.

We can easily steal this "inconvenient truth" line from [former vice president and environmental activist] Al Gore: It's a seriously inconvenient truth for Hollywood that they have been pressed, prodded and preached, and finally it took federal legislation, in the form of massive potential fines, to get their attention.

It would have been preferable to leave the government out of this popular-culture equation, but it came down to federal intervention after Hollywood's absolute refusal to live up to its stated commitment at self-regulation. The networks' offerings of a ratings system and V-chip were as fatally flawed as they were calculated: Hollywood knew these would do nothing to protect children from the barrage of filth that Hollywood is dumping on the public airwaves right in front of impressionable youngsters. The V-chip relies on the flawed ratings system. The ratings are inconsistent, inaccurate, arbitrary and unreliable, not just across the various networks but even within networks themselves. Parents simply cannot rely on these to protect their children.

Self-Regulation Does Not Work

It's important to state [that] this bill Bush signed does not change in any way the current broadcasting decency standards. It only increases the potential fines for egregious violations, like strip teases during Super Bowls, deliberate droppings of the "f-bomb," and the like. Just about anything short of that will fail to trip the sensors at the FCC [Federal Communications Commission]. Turn on your TV tonight and you'll find the broadcast airwaves filled with filth, garbage rising right to the line, but not over that line, that could trigger a penalty.

That's Hollywood's commitment to self-regulation for you.

And how's this for that commitment to self-regulation: The four largest networks and 800 of their affiliates quietly have gone to court demanding the right to air the f-word and the s-word on the public airwaves any time and anywhere they wish, no matter how many children are watching.

CBS is going even further. After the Janet Jackson striptease [during the 2004 Super Bowl halftime show on CBS, Jackson's breast was briefly exposed], the head of CBS was hauled before Congress to explain himself. After apologizing for violating the public trust, this man announced to great fanfare that CBS now had a "zero-tolerance policy" toward indecency. That same network has now gone to court to appeal the subsequent half-million dollar fine it incurred, now arguing there's nothing indecent about a woman stripping off her clothes in front of tens of millions of impressionable children during the Super Bowl. That's self-regulation, Hollywood style.

Ultimately, the massive increase in potential federal fines became a reality for one reason, and one reason only: Hollywood cannot be taken at its word.

> *"The good news is that the free speech zone outside the FCC's dominion keeps growing."*

The Government Should Not Strictly Regulate Indecency on Television

Jesse Walker

Jesse Walker is the managing editor of Reason *magazine and Reason.com. In the following viewpoint, he maintains that the Federal Communications Commission (FCC) is fighting a futile battle over indecency; while cable television or Internet programming can broadcast indecent language and behaviors, network television is subject to draconian fines. Walker argues that the FCC would be well served by relaxing the indecency regulations and fines.*

As you read, consider the following questions:

1. According to the author, what curse did Bono utter at the Golden Globes in 2003, which was broadcast on network television?

2. According to Walker, how did the FCC treat indecency on network television in the 1990s?

3. According to the author, what was Supreme Court justice Clarence Thomas's concurring opinion on a recent FCC case?

On December 9, 2002, Cher received a lifetime achievement trophy at the Billboard Music Awards. Overcome with emotion, the Armenian-American singer noted that she had faced "critics for the last 40 years saying that I was on my way out every year." Then she added, "F--- 'em." Fox broadcast the scene live, f-bomb and all.

So began an epidemic of unexpected expletives at award shows. A month later, as NBC transmitted the Golden Globes, the singer/lobbyist Bono announced that his Best Song prize was "really, really f---ing brilliant." And in December 2003, when the Billboard Music Awards came on Fox again, the reality TV star Nicole Richie asked the audience, "Have you ever tried to get cow shit out of a Prada purse? It's not so f---ing simple."

The FCC Reacts

Before the contagion could spread, the Federal Communications Commission [FCC] stepped in. After initially announcing that Bono's comment was acceptable—his phrase "may be crude and offensive," the regulators had declared, "but, in the context presented here, did not describe sexual or excretory organs or activities"—the agency reversed itself, ruling that broadcasters could be fined for airing even fleeting, unplanned cussing at live events. The f-word, it explained, was "one of the most vulgar, graphic, and explicit words for sexual activity in the English language," and there was no place for it on television.

No place, that is, except the hundreds of channels that the content cops weren't allowed to regulate. When it came to "indecent" images and language, the [George W.] Bush–era FCC toughened its rules, increased its fines, and stepped up its enforcement, but the commission's grip on mass communications wasn't as complete as it used to be; as cable and then the Internet exploded, the area outside the indecency police's grasp was growing. Like the sheriff of a dry county surrounded by rowdy biker bars, the FCC could make life miserable for the people under its jurisdiction but it couldn't do a thing about what was going on right next door.

The crackdown was bipartisan—the noisiest censor at the commission, Michael Copps, is a Democrat—but it was a post–[Bill] Clinton development. In the '90s the networks had started to behave as though they had the same liberties as their cable competitors: You could hear the word "piss" on *Northern Exposure*, see Dennis Franz's bare butt on *NYPD Blue*, watch *Schindler's List*—naked bodies and all—prime time on NBC. In 1997, when then-congressman Tom Coburn complained about the latter program's "full-frontal nudity, violence, and profanity," he was roundly mocked for treating an earnest Holocaust drama like it was *Ilsa, She-Wolf of the SS*. In 2004, by contrast, after the clampdown was underway, several ABC affiliates refused to air an equally earnest Spielberg picture, the World War II drama *Saving Private Ryan*. In a model example of a chilling effect, the stations feared the government would fine them for the film's rough language.

Viewers Find Alternatives

Yet while the FCC was reasserting control of its corner of the media, audiences were exiting in ever-greater numbers for non-network news and entertainment. If you wanted to see a singing turd on *South Park*, or Tony Soprano [from *The Sopranos*] screwing a stripper in a back room at the Bing, or a bestiality film on a fetish site—well, there wasn't anything the commission could do about that. But a fleeting expletive at an awards show: *That* was fair game.

Whether it stays fair game is another matter. After the commission declared that Cher-style vulgarity was verboten

[forbidden], the major broadcast networks jointly filed a suit to stop the policy. Their case has been bopping up and down the courts for several years now. This week [May 1, 2009,] the U.S. Supreme Court refused to accept a procedural argument against the FCC's orders, but the justices left the door open to later declaring the rules an unconstitutional infringement on speech. For now the legal battle will return to the 2nd U.S. Circuit Court of Appeals in New York, from where it will probably crawl back up to the Supremes.

Emphasizing Free Speech

When the justices wrote their reactions to the case, some of the sharpest comments came in Clarence Thomas's concurring opinion. While siding with the commission on the technical legal question immediately at hand, Thomas signaled his sympathy with the argument that the rules violate the First Amendment. The two precedents that supported the FCC's authority—1969's *Red Lion* decision, which upheld the Fairness Doctrine, and 1978's *Pacifica* decision, which upheld the government's right to restrict indecent language—"were unconvincing when they were issued," Thomas wrote, "and the passage of time has only increased doubt regarding their continued validity." He continued:

> Broadcast spectrum is significantly less scarce than it was 40 years ago. . . . Moreover, traditional broadcast television and radio are no longer the "uniquely pervasive" media forms they once were. For most consumers, traditional broadcast media programming is now bundled with cable or satellite services. . . . Broadcast and other video programming is also widely available over the Internet. . . . And like radio and television broadcasts, Internet access is now often freely available over the airwaves and can be accessed by portable computer, cell phones, and other wireless devices. . . . The extant facts that drove this Court to subject broadcasters to unique disfavor under the First Amendment simply do not exist today.

There is no credible reason we shouldn't have the same right to free expression on the FM and VHF bands that we have when using WiFi or cable. Now, there are those in the commission, the courts, and the Congress who would resolve the contradiction by extending the indecency rules' reach to cable and cyberspace. But if the courts respect the language of the First Amendment, they'll extend the reach of free speech instead.

In the meantime, the FCC is simultaneously empowered and impotent, an agency reduced to chasing passing curse words on network TV while cable subscribers enjoy unhindered access to Spice and the Playboy Channel. The bad news is that the courts might tell the commission it's within its rights when it censors the networks. The good news is that the free speech zone outside the FCC's dominion keeps growing.

> *"Graphic violent programming has be-
> come so pervasive and has been shown
> to be so harmful, we are left with no
> choice but to have the government step
> in."*

The Government Should Strictly Regulate Television Violence

John D. Rockefeller IV

John D. Rockefeller IV is a US senator from West Virginia and chairman of the Senate Committee on Commerce, Science, and Transportation. In the following testimony on a hearing on the effect of media violence on children, he contends that children are being subjected to an unprecedented level of television vio-lence and the government must do a better job of imposing regu-lations on limits of television violence.

As you read, consider the following questions:

1. Who does Rockefeller hold responsible for the rising level of television violence?

John D. Rockefeller IV, "Impact of Media Violence on Children," U.S. Senate Committee on Commerce, Science & Transportation, June 26, 2007. Copyright © 2007 by U.S. Sen-ate Committee on Commerce, Science and Transportation. Reproduced by permission.

2. According to the author, how many hours a day do children watch television?

3. How many murders, rapes, and assaults each year does the average American youth see on television, according to Rockefeller?

The issue of protecting children from indecent, violent, and profane content is a deeply personal and important issue to me. Last Congress, I introduced legislation to address this issue, and will do so again in the coming weeks.

After years of inadequate and ineffective voluntary efforts by the industry, we are no closer to solving the problem of indecent and violent programming for children despite claims that parents have many tools at their disposal to address unwanted programming.

Children today are being subjected to an unprecedented level of violent television content. There is no doubt it is coarsening our culture. I fear, too, that it is weakening our society.

For too long, we have heard promises to do better, to put better tools in the hands of parents, to provide more options for families. But none of this has yielded results. Instead, we have the industry blaming parents for their lack of oversight of children's television viewing. This is cowardly. We have a responsibility to do better, a responsibility the government must take seriously.

Disturbing Images

I hold the entertainment industry responsible. Decades of scientific research have shown that violent television programming has a detrimental impact on the development of children. Yet today the content industry is in a neverending race to the bottom. It makes you wonder if there even is a bottom anymore.

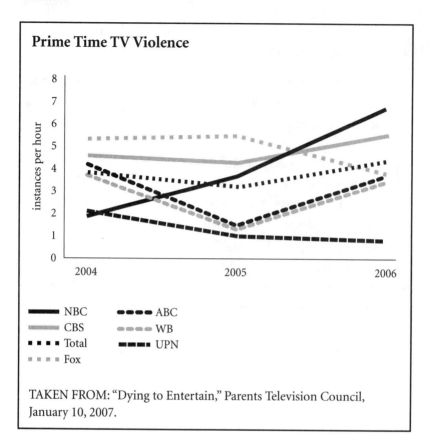

Prime Time TV Violence

instances per hour

8
7
6
5
4
3
2
1
0

2004   2005   2006

——— NBC   ●●●● ABC
▬▬▬ CBS   ● ● ● WB
▪ ▪ ▪ Total   ▬▪▬▪ UPN
▪ ▪ ▪ Fox

TAKEN FROM: "Dying to Entertain," Parents Television Council, January 10, 2007.

I am not sure that all of my colleagues know how violent television has become. At my request, the Parents Television Council has put together a CD with clips from broadcast and cable channels that show shocking, violent images. These images are inherently disturbing to adults so we can only imagine their impact on children.

I know some of our witnesses will go into far greater detail, but let us consider these facts

- Children watch on average between two and four hours of television every day;

- The occurrence of violence on television has increased by 75% since 1998 and has increased across the board on all five of the major broadcast networks;

- On average, American youth view more than 1,000 murders, rapes, and assaults each year on television.

- Sadly, by the time our children leave elementary school, they will have seen on average 100,000 acts of violence on television.

When I am home, I meet with West Virginia parents and educators and they have told me that children's behavior is becoming more aggressive and at times crude or explicit, and that they blame television for much of the problem.

Violence Sells

I have met with many representatives from the entertainment industry representing broadcasters, cable, movies, and others. The one thing every CEO [chief executive officer] I meet tells me is that they are personally appalled by the violent content that is on television and they personally . . . agree with me. And, if they could change it they [w]ould. But yet, I never get a reason as to why the industry will not stop showing violent content. I think we all know the answer. Violent content is cheap to produce and profitable. It sells.

The entertainment industry could change what we watch on television but it chooses to sell sex and violence instead. I reject the notion that television merely reflects our society, but rather I believe that television can and should be a positive force.

To be blunt, the big media companies have placed a greater emphasis on their corporate short term profits than on the long term health and well being of our children.

Time to Take Responsibility

Instead of addressing the problem—too much violent programming on television—the industry seeks to hide behind ineffective band aids of voluntary action and providing parents more "tools". Parents do not want more tools. They want the content off the air.

It is no big secret that the industry has hoped that its latest voluntary campaign will stave off Congress from establishing common sense content and ratings regulations for television. I know that we will hear their now familiar arguments here today. The entertainment industry will claim that voluntary actions are sufficient and that they are only giving the public what it wants to view while giving parents all the tools necessary to block unwanted programming.

But, none of these arguments are persuasive enough to convince me to abandon a serious effort to protect children from unconscionable levels of sex and gratuitous violence, on what, remains the most pervasive inescapable means of communication in America today—television.

TV Networks Cannot Self-Regulate

We now know that the entertainment and broadcasting industry has proven itself unable and unwilling to police itself.

I fear that graphic violent programming has become so pervasive and has been shown to be so harmful, we are left with no choice but to have the government step in.

I know that Congress has been reluctant to take on the issue of violence because defining decency is difficult. I will again reintroduce my legislation, because we must address this issue. I understand that these are hard lines to draw, but just because they are difficult doesn't mean that we should stand by and do nothing. For the sake of our children and grandchildren, we have a moral obligation to tackle television violence and arm our parents with the tools to make their children safer.

The real question for all of us here today is "What are we going to do about protecting our children from the pervasive and escalating level of television violence?" Doing nothing is not an option.

> *"Be wary of people, especially people in government, who would upend adult rights with proposals couched in the language of protecting children."*

The Government Should Not Strictly Regulate Television Violence

Jack Shafer

Jack Shafer is an editor at large for Slate, *an online periodical. In the following viewpoint, he expresses his wariness at expanding the oversight powers of the Federal Communications Commission (FCC) to more strictly regulate television violence. Shafer argues that if parents are worried about their children's television viewing habits, they should monitor it themselves—not leave it to the government.*

As you read, consider the following questions:

1. According to a 2004 Kaiser Family Foundation study cited by the author, what percentage of parents who know they have V-chip technology, have ever used it?

2. What does Shafer argue is needed before even thinking of expanding the FCC's regulatory powers?

3. According to the author, what did experts believe about gangster movies in the 1930s?

When the government announces a desire to "protect" children, what it's usually got on its mind is new ways of controlling adults.

In response to a request from members of Congress, the Federal Communications Commission [FCC, in April 2007] released its study of the effects of violent television programming on children and the legal feasibility of regulating such content.

V-Chip Controversy

The study confesses that the FCC's previous interventions designed to shield children from violent content have failed spectacularly. Since 2000, all new televisions with screens 13 inches and larger have had to include FCC mandated V-chips that read the "voluntary" rating applied to programs by producers. (The "V" stands for "violence.") By manipulating V-chip settings, parents can block programs they deem too violent, too sexual, or too crude for their children to watch. A survey by the Kaiser Family Foundation published in 2004 found that only 20 percent of parents who know they have a V-chip-capable set have ever used the technology. That number is probably high. In a *Slate* piece, Thomas Hazlett recounts a study in which 110 families with children were given new V-chipped TV sets, and most got extensive operating instructions. At the end of one year, 77 families reported that they'd never tried the device, while just 8 percent claimed to be using it.

Rather than interpreting the general snubbing of the V-chip as a cue that parents don't yearn for greater government participation in their viewing schedules, the FCC concludes that the V-chip system—which it designed—is "of limited effectiveness in protecting children from violent television content." The FCC study indicates that the V-chip is too hard to use, too hidden from users, and the "voluntary" ratings system too forgiving of violent and sexual content to be good screening agents. The FCC notes one unintended consequence of the "voluntary" ratings system: Some young viewers rely on them to find explicitly sexual and violent programs. It's "Daddy, I really want to see that R-rated movie" all over again.

Expanding FCC Power

When Rep. Joe Barton, R-Texas, and 38 other House [of Representatives] members contacted the FCC, they wanted its opinion of whether legislation restricting excessively violent programming could be written that would pass constitutional review. Not a problem, replies the FCC, citing the laws and regulations that sequester sexually explicit or "indecent" programming into the 10 PM-to-6 AM "safe harbor" in the name of protecting children. The commission continues:

> We also believe that, if properly defined, excessively violent programming, like indecent programming, occupies a relatively low position in the hierarchy of First Amendment values because it is of "slight social value as a step to truth."

The commission concludes that, oh yes, let's expand the FCC's power to regulate broadcaster content with a new law, but cautions Congress on the difficulty of actually defining excessive violence. One person's example of gratuitous media violence is another person's idea of a film classic, a fantastic war documentary, or a brilliant newscast from an urban riot. But far from being daunted by the perpetual needlework of OK'ing one kind of violence because it's artistic, historical, or newsworthy but nixing another as too wanton, the FCC appears to relish the idea of refereeing all television programming everywhere. Imagine that, a federal agency keen on increasing its oversight powers!

Supreme Court Weighs In

The Supreme Court decided in *FCC v. Pacifica Foundation* that the government could regulate "indecent" broadcasts because the medium was "uniquely pervasive," that is, broadcasts "extend into the privacy of the home and it is impossible completely to avoid." (What, no off switches on those radios and televisions?) The cherry on the top of the Supreme Court's decision was that broadcasts were "uniquely accessible to children."

The only reason broadcasts are "pervasive" is because the government, which sets the technical standards for broadcasters and TV sets, has made them so. Cable television, on the other hand, isn't pervasive. You've got to invite it into your house. Want to avoid it? Stop paying for it. Cable, therefore, escapes the Supreme Court's decency standards, which would leave one to expect the FCC to exclude cable from its regulation of media violence discussion. But no. The report suggests that viewers be given the option of subscribing to an "a la carte" selection of cable TV channels, instead of bundled channels, as a strategy for keeping violent programs out of the home. Presumably, mandated a la carte would put the FCC back in the business of determining cable TV rates. Imagine that, a federal agency keen on increasing its oversight powers!

Better Research Is Needed

Before we even think of expanding the FCC's regulatory powers, we need a better study of the effects of violence on children than this report offers. In its review of the literature, the report concludes, "We agree with the views of the Surgeon General and find that, on balance, research provides strong evidence that exposure to violence in the media *can* increase aggressive behavior in children, at least *in the short term.*" [Emphasis added.] A clear and present danger, this is not.

Not all media violence is created equal, an obvious observation that David Trend offers in his thorough book *The Myth*

Regulation Will Not Work

The FCC [Federal Communications Commission] is ... going to have a hard time convincing the courts why pervasiveness-based rationales for TV regulation make sense in a world of media abundance. Has the FCC heard of the Internet, YouTube, iPods, PlayStation Portables, and cell phones? Most kids have, and that's increasingly where they watch TV shows today.

Adam D. Theirer,
"Should We Regulate Violent TV?"
City Journal, *April 30, 2007.*

of Media Violence. Is the violence on-screen or off? What type of character committed the violence, and why? What are the consequences of the violence? Is the violence justified? Does it cause pain or suffering? Does the violent character reap his just rewards? Do we sympathize with the victim? Who is the intended audience? Is computer-generated movie violence more abhorrent than violence produced with conventional effects? Is it "burlesque violence" or "retaliatory violence"? Is animal-on-animal violence to be avoided? How about violence on the news? Is mock violence that is inspired by a TV show violence, too? Professional boxing: violence or sport?

Solutions More Troubling than Problems

Trend notes that every media age brings forth violent entertainments that both repulse and attract. "Victorian-era street theater and penny novels were thought to encourage misbehavior among the working poor, especially young men in urban areas." Gangster movies in the 1930s were said to increase violence, as were comic books in the 1950s. Rap music and video games, likewise, have been accused of teaching kids to kill, although crime statistics don't support that assertion.

Anybody who has children—or was once a child—won't flippantly dismiss the question of whether TV violence is an issue worthy of study and debate. But be wary of people, especially people in government, who would upend adult rights with proposals couched in the language of protecting children. The only way to protect children from every possible injury is to infantilize our world.

Never mind the problem of TV violence for a moment. Please protect me from the solutions.

> *"I'm betting if we ran a poll . . . , we'd have a landslide win on wanting [government] intervention to turn the ads down."*

The Government Should Regulate the Volume Levels of Television Commercials

Bruce Simmons

Bruce Simmons is a contributor to Screen Rant, a website featuring television and movie news and reviews. In the following viewpoint, he finds it odd that the Federal Communications Commission (FCC) does not regulate the volume of television commercials, noting that it is a long-standing and common problem for many television viewers.

As you read, consider the following questions:

1. According to Simmons, what excuse do television networks give to consumers about loud television commercials?

2. Who is working on legislation to address the television ad issue, according to the author?

3. Why, according to Simmons, would there be opposition to a bill regulating the volume of television commercials?

Back in the '08 I vented about how loud TV ads are. I had conducted a little research and discovered the fluffy excuse that networks give the consumers: They aren't louder, they only sound louder.

You have got to be &%$#ing kidding me? They call it "signal compression" which amplifies certain aspects of a signal. And if you didn't feel insulted enough, there is always this one: Ads seem loud because they come on during the quietest moments.

Wow, they must think I'm some kind of simpleton who believes everything they read on the internet or believes in all those commercials I get pounded with.

Back on Track

An ad can't be any louder than the loudest part of the television program it's being played in.

To a tiny extent, I understand their lame excuse about compression. I used to have to play with my bass and treble on my stereo so I could play it louder, but not have the "mini concerts" in my apartment bother my neighbors.

Networks on the other hand tamper with the settings so all the neighbors can hear them, not just you, but despite continual waves of complaints, the FCC [Federal Communications Commission] does not regulate television volume. I find that rather odd considering the commercial volume has been a common issue for, like, ever!

Is Anyone on Your Side?

It doesn't feel like it. Well, you can count me in. Of late, I'm also feeling like ads are playing longer during the hour than they used to, but I haven't sat down and timed them yet.

I know readers of *Screen Rant*, people I know have sworn off paying for TV and instead, pay for the DVD's that have no commercials just because of the intrusions and annoyances that commercials represent. I'm almost on that band wagon also. Dang . . . they're everywhere, including in-screen.

Since the FCC Has Not Stepped In . . .

Since the FCC has kept a hands-off kind of attitude, for whatever reason, others have stepped up: Rep. Anna Eshoo [D-California] and Sen. Sheldon Whitehouse [D-Rhode Island] are working to smother the TV ad volume issue.

They've submitted the Commercial Advertisement Loudness Mitigation Act. (CALM). With 62 co-sponsors from Eshoo, the bill passed the House Subcommittee on Communications, Technology and the Internet. (Sheesh, could they have given that a longer name?)

Now we wait to see when the Senate will take the time to review the bill. Oddly, there's opposition to the premise. What the flipnut!?

One of my reference articles from a blog called *The Hill* questions if it's the right use of time by Congress or the FCC to deal with such an issue, what with them presently working on a broadband plan and net neutrality regulations—this would distract from that.

And then it's also questioned whether or not consumers want additional government interference with their TV sets. What in blazes have we been complaining about all these years? That question just blows me out of the water.

I'm betting if we ran a poll here on *Screen Rant*, we'd have a landslide win on wanting intervention to turn the ads down.

My source ends by saying that after the digital transition and all the issues, *"many of them are probably so thrilled to get a digital signal at all, they don't mind the commercials. Loud or not."*

Crickets . . . lots and lots of crickets.

Too Loud

If you aren't involved in watching television as much as some, I understand where folks are coming from. They're focused on the economy, the war and various other social issues.

But there are those that television is their hobby, their time to wind down. And we want to do that without being traumatized by mega loud ads that give us ringing ears for a week.

Dare I ask ... but does everyone agree, that commercials are too loud?

> *"The CALM Act would address 'volume manipulation' in TV ads. . . . Clearly, this is valuable use of our regulators' time."*

The Government Should Not Regulate the Volume Levels of Television Commercials

Adam Thierer

Adam Thierer is the president of the Progress & Freedom Foundation, a digital economy think tank and the author of several books on technology and media policy. In the following viewpoint, he ridicules the government's recent efforts to regulate the volume levels of television ads and product placements in television shows. Thierer argues that US tax dollars and regulators' time can be put to better use.

As you read, consider the following questions:

1. What is the C.A.L.M. Act, according to the author?

2. According to Thierer, what is product placement?

3. What does the author believe attempts at regulations will conflict with?

Adam Thierer, "Regulators to Save Us from Loud TV Ads and Product Placements," *The Technology Liberation Front*, June 24, 2008. Copyright © 2008 by Technology Liberation Front. Reproduced by permission of the author.

Couch potatoes of America, have no fear—our friendly neighborhood super-regulators are about to swoop in and save you from the scourge of loud TV ads and "illegal" product placements! As we all learned in our high school Civics 101 classes, this is why the American Revolution was fought: We Americans have an unambiguous constitutional birthright to be free of the tyranny of "excessive loudness" during commercial breaks; and pesky product promos during our favorite network dramas. (Seriously, it's right there in the footnotes to the Bill of Rights; you probably just missed it before.)

The C.A.L.M. Act

Rep. Anna Eshoo (D-Calif.) has the first problem covered. She and her House colleague Rep. Zoe Lofgren (D-Calif.) are proposing H.R. 6209, the "Commercial Advertisement Loudness Mitigation Act." (Oh, isn't that so cute! The "C.A.L.M. Act"! How very, very witty.) The CALM Act would address "volume manipulation" in TV ads by making sure that TV ads are not "excessively noisy or strident." (Strident! We Americans hate "strident" ads.) The bill would empower regulators at the Federal Communications Commission [FCC] to take steps to ensure that "such advertisements shall not be presented at modulation levels substantially higher than the program material that such advertisements accompany; and, the average maximum loudness of such advertisements shall not be substantially higher than the average maximum loudness of the program material that such advertisements accompany."

Clearly, this is valuable use of our regulators' time. I look forward to the day when I can visit the FCC and see my tax dollars at work as teams of bureaucrats closely monitor each episode of *Desperate Housewives* and *Swingtown* in search of such malicious volume manipulation during the commercial breaks. (Incidentally, where is the form I need to fill out to get that job? Heck, I'll take minimum wage pay to do this all day long.)

Another Problem Addressed

So, we can rest easier now know[ing] that lawmakers will take care of this egregious violation of our human rights. But what about the potential product placements in various TV dramas or comedies? Luckily, the folks at the FCC are on it. According to *Reuters*:

> U.S. regulators are expected to take the first step this week that could rein in advertisers' growing use of product placements on television shows, two sources close to the agency told Reuters on Monday [June 2008]. The Federal Communications Commission will vote to study whether TV shows should carry more conspicuous notices informing viewers when advertisers paid to have food, automobiles and other products prominently displayed during programs, the sources said.

Thank God, our long national nightmare is over! Never again will we have to see another *Seinfeld* rerun where Jerry just stands there mocking our sensibilities with a Coca-Cola can in his hand! And thank God our regulators will be freeing us from the frightful sight of a Ford Mustang in the staring role of the remake of *Knight Rider*. I mean, what an insult to the original K.I.T.T.! Have they no shame!

"Baptist and Bootleggers" Affair

Apparently, the anti-product placement movement is a true "baptist and bootleggers" affair. This righteous crusade features a strange bedfellows coalition of Lefties and social conservatives who [are] all hell-bent on saving us from the evils of commercial advertising. "We must not allow television programs to become Trojan horses, carrying messages that would otherwise be criticized by the public or even deemed illegal," wrote members of this coalition, which includes Public Citizen and the Parents Television Council [PTC]. (Thank you Public Citizen and PTC for forcing us to spend our taxpayer money on this regulatory effort! I'm glad you're looking out for our best interests since most of us are not capable of doing so on our own.)

What remains unclear about both the CALM Act and the effort to regulate product placement, however, is how it conflicts with our other unambiguous constitutional right to all the free or cheap TV that we please! Someone needs to pay for all that content, after all, but it sure in hell ain't going to be us, right? I mean, how dare they subject to us to loud ads or product placements in an attempt to get us to pay attention to the ads we are busy skipping with our TiVos [digital video recorders]!

Government Focuses on the Important Issues

Evil, evil people in the media business, I tell you! Our benevolent leaders on high must save us from this scourge and put a stop to all this. And don't worry about the availability of free or cheap TV. It will continue to just fall like manna from heaven in our laps, without any commercial interruption. Or, if not, I guess we could always just watch commercial-free public television all day long. Yeah, that's the ticket—bring on a 24/7 lineup of *Antiques Roadshow* and *Victory Garden*, all gloriously free of the evils of commercialism that is corrupting of our fragile little minds!

We are so repressed. Down with commercialism! Down with capitalism! Down with THE MAN!

Periodical Bibliography

The following articles have been selected to supplement the diverse views presented in this chapter.

Debbie Blair	"FCC Condoning Television Indecency," *San Diego Union-Tribune*, April 1, 2010.
L. Brent Bozell III	"Disturbing TV Violence, Unchecked," Media Research Center, June 1, 2007. www.mediaresearch.org.
Steve Chapman	"The FCC's F-Word: Freedom," Townhall.com, April 30, 2009.
Christian Science Monitor	"FCC Must Appeal Ruling Against Its Indecency Regulations," July 15, 2010.
Cecilia Kang	"Court Rules Against the FCC Policies on Indecency," *Washington Post*, July 14, 2010.
Los Angeles Times	"The FCC's Decency Dilemma," July 14, 2010.
Simon Mann	"Court Overturns Ban on Expletives," *Age*, July 16, 2010.
Providence (RI) Journal	"New Leeway for Broadcasters," July 26, 2010.
Peter Suderman	"Flipping Off the FCC," *National Review*, June 11, 2007.
Jacob Sullum	"The Mystery of Violence," *Reason*, May 16, 2007. www.reason.com.
Nick Summers	"Now Can I Say $*%@!#& on Television?" *Newsweek*, July 26, 2010.
Adam D. Thierer	"Should We Regulate Violent TV?" *City Journal*, April 30, 2007.
Edward Wyatt	"FCC Indecency Policy Rejected on Appeal," *New York Times*, July 13, 2010.

For Further Discussion

Chapter 1

1. Anna Stewart and Dinesh D'Souza disagree about television's relationship to society and its values. Do you believe that television reflects societal values? Why or why not?

2. In his viewpoint, Greg Beato argues that there are plenty of family-friendly television programs today. L. Brent Bozell III counters that view, maintaining that television is becoming more indecent and less family friendly. In your opinion, is television becoming more or less family friendly? Explain your answer, citing from the viewpoints.

3. With growing numbers of gay characters on television, concerns have arisen that many of these programs just reinforce gay stereotypes. Ramin Setoodeh and Kevin Hilke disagree on the topic. After reading their viewpoints, do you think that gay characters on television reinforce negative gay stereotypes? Why or why not?

4. Torture has been a controversial issue in the past few years. Dahlia Lithwick asserts that television programs like *24* promote torture and have an impact on government policy and public opinion. Chris Barsanti maintains that such programs are much more nuanced than given credit for and reflect the national debate on torture. What do you think about the portrayal of torture on television programs like *24*?

Chapter 2

1. Reality shows have been a growing trend on network and cable television. In her view, Colleen Carroll Campbell finds these programs exploitative, while Emili Johnson

argues that reality television should be regarded for what it is: escapist entertainment. How do you perceive reality television after reading their viewpoints?

2. Explaining the value of reality television, Michael Hirschorn contends that it addresses hot-button issues such as sexuality and greed. In his viewpoint, Jonah Goldberg concludes that it has no redeeming value and debases society. Do you think reality television has any redeeming values? What are they, if you do, and if you do not, why not? If you have a favorite reality television program, what issues does it address? If you do not, explain why not.

3. James Parker views prison programs like *Lockup* to be insightful and educational. Dawn K. Cecil and Jennifer L. Leitner argue that such programs offer a distorted view of the prison experience. What can viewers learn about the prison experience from such shows? Or do you believe the shows provide an inaccurate perspective on prison life? Explain your answer.

Chapter 3

1. Do you think television ads have become more indecent? Or do they reflect societal values? Cite the viewpoints by Nathan Hoofnel and Linda Chavez when explaining your position.

2. In the past few years, advocacy ads have generated controversy and offended some groups. There has been debate over when they should be aired and what standards should be applied to them. In a pair of viewpoints, Tracy Clark-Flory and Jeffrey Lord illuminate the issues involved in the debate. Which viewpoint do you find represents your position and why?

3. Infomercials are all the rage on television lately. Matthew Maudlin asserts that infomercials are very effective, while John Jacobs criticizes the form for taking advantage of the

gullible and bored. What is your view of infomercials? Do you believe that they are an effective mode of advertising? Explain your answer.

4. The popularity of the digital video recorder (DVR) and its impact on advertising is debated in a pair of viewpoints written by *BusinessWeek* and PR Newswire. After reading both viewpoints, which prediction do you think is more accurate? How do you think DVRs will ultimately affect television ads?

Chapter 4

1. Many of the most controversial issues surrounding the Federal Communications Commission (FCC) center on its regulation of indecency and network television programming. In his viewpoint, L. Brent Bozell III contends that the FCC should have more power to fine networks that air offensive television programs. Jesse Walker, however, argues that the FCC should be less concerned with fining for every dirty or offensive word. What do you think should be the parameters of the FCC's role in this area? Explain your answer using past controversial incidents mentioned in the viewpoints.

2. Violence is another controversial issue for the FCC. John D. Rockefeller IV maintains that excessive violence has a negative impact on children and therefore should be strictly regulated by the FCC. Jack Shafer argues that it is not the FCC's job to monitor the amount of violence on television. Which view do you agree with and why?

Organizations to Contact

The editors have compiled the following list of organizations concerned with the issues debated in this book. The descriptions are derived from materials provided by the organizations. All have publications or information available for interested readers. The list was compiled on the date of publication of the present volume; the information provided here may change. Be aware that many organizations take several weeks or longer to respond to inquiries, so allow as much time as possible.

Academy of Television Arts & Sciences (ATAS)
5220 Lankershim Blvd., North Hollywood, CA   91601
(818) 754-2800 • fax: (818) 761-2827
website: www.emmys.tv

The Academy of Television Arts & Sciences is a nonprofit organization created to advance telecommunications arts and sciences and to foster creative leadership in the television industry. It is made up of performers, directors, producers, art directors, technicians, and television executives. ATAS is responsible for the annual Primetime Emmy Awards, which recognizes excellence in television programming. The organization also publishes *Emmy Magazine*, which covers a range of topics ranging from current programming and artist profiles to political and social issues that impact the industry, like censorship and free-speech controversies.

Ad Council
815 Second Ave., 9th Fl., New York, NY   10017
(212) 922-1500
website: www.adcouncil.org

The Ad Council produces and distributes public service announcements (PSAs) by utilizing the skills and talents of volunteers from the advertising and communications industries, the media, and the business and nonprofit communities. PSAs are public service ads broadcast on network television and radio that aim to educate the public on issues of health and welfare and improve the lives of Americans, especially children. Many of the Ad Council's PSAs, as well as research on the impact of its campaigns and audience studies, can be found on the council's website.

American Civil Liberties Union (ACLU)

125 Broad St., 18th Fl., New York, NY   10004
(212) 549-2500
website: www.aclu.org

The American Civil Liberties Union is a civil liberties organization that works to protect and extend the rights of all Americans, particularly First Amendment rights, equal protection under the law, the right to due process, and the right to privacy. The ACLU fights against such issues as racism, sexism, homophobia, religious intolerance, and censorship. The ACLU has often tangled with the Federal Communications Commission in order to push back against censorship and support free speech and free expression on television and the Internet. On its website, the ACLU posts video, podcasts, games, documents, reports, and speech transcripts, as well as news and commentary on censorship and free-speech issues. The ACLU also offers a blog and in-depth reports on related issues.

Federal Communications Commission (FCC)

445 Twelfth St. SW, Washington, DC   20554
(888) 225-5322 • fax: (866) 418-0232
e-mail: fccinfo@fcc.gov
website: www.fcc.gov

Established in 1934, the Federal Communications Commission is an independent US government agency that regulates radio, television, wire, satellite, and cable communications. The FCC issues and revokes broadcasting licenses, enforces the Communications Act, and fines violators of the act's provisions. The FCC proposes regulations to protect the American people and the telecommunications industry. Citizens can use the FCC website to file complaints about television programs or personalities.

Media Matters for America

445 Massachusetts Ave. NW, Ste. 600, Washington, DC   20001
(202) 756-4100
website: www.mediamatters.org

Media Matters for America is a web-based nonprofit research organization that works to monitor and correct conservative misinformation in print, television, radio, and the Internet. It accomplishes this through opinion pieces, research, and in-depth studies of conservative programming and current issues of interest. The Media Matters website, features a blog to address breaking issues, video clips of instances of conservative misinformation, and the organization's own programming to analyze pertinent stories. It also publishes a number of newsletters and media alerts that offer readers the latest news and updates on relevant stories.

Media Research Center (MRC)

325 S. Patrick St., Alexandria, VA   22314
(703) 683-9733 • fax: (703) 683-9736
website: www.mrc.org

The Media Research Center is a conservative watchdog group that monitors media, particularly television, for a liberal bias. Its aim is to expose and eliminate liberal leanings in television news programming. MRC publishes the opinion columns and studies of L. Brent Bozell III, its president and founder, as well as scientific research to back its claims of a pervasive liberal bias in mainstream media. The MRC website features a blog to address breaking issues, video clips of television shows, and the group's own programming to analyze pertinent stories. MRC also publishes a number of newsletters that offer readers in-depth studies and research on liberal media bias.

National Cable & Telecommunications Association (NCTA)
25 Massachusetts Ave. NW, Ste. 100
Washington, DC   20001-1413
(202) 222-2300
website: www.ncta.com

Established in 1952, the National Cable & Telecommunications Association is the principal trade association of the cable television industry of the United States. It advocates sound policy in the cable and telecommunications industry. It hosts a number of events—such as conferences, seminars, and conventions—and disseminates the latest policy and industry news to its members. NCTA also organizes the Vanguard Awards, which rewards excellence in the cable and telecommunications industry.

National Coalition Against Censorship (NCAC)
275 Seventh Ave., Ste. 1504, New York, NY   10001
(212) 807-6222 • fax: (212) 807-6245
e-mail: ncac@ncac.org
website: www.ncac.org

The National Coalition Against Censorship is a network of fifty-two participating organizations that work together to support freedom of expression. NCAC accomplishes this through disseminating educational resources, offering support to individuals and organizations affected by censorship, documenting incidents of censorship, and lobbying the media and public about the dangers of censorship. NCAC also provides research and studies on censorship issues, and publishes a quarterly newsletter, *NCAC Censorship News*, that discusses current school censorship controversies, policies, and obscenity laws.

Parents Television Council (PTC)
707 Wilshire Blvd., Ste. 2075, Los Angeles, CA   90017
(800) 882-6868 • fax: (213) 403-1301
e-mail: editor@parentstv.org
website: www.parentstv.org

The Parents Television Council is an organization that aims to educate parents on television content so they can make informed television-viewing decisions. It monitors television programs for excessive violence, sexual content, and indecent language and rates each program for easy reference. PTC publishes the *Family Guide to Primetime Television* and *PTC Picks* for concerned parents and viewers in search of family-friendly television, as well as the monthly *PTC Insider* newsletter. It also publishes in-depth studies on specific issues, such as the prevalence of violence on television, representations of marriage on specific programs, and violence against women in many television storylines. The PTC website features weekly columns providing commentary on current controversies.

Bibliography of Books

Jonathan Bignell — *Big Brother: Reality TV in the Twenty-First Century.* New York: Palgrave Macmillan, 2005.

David S. Escoffery, ed. — *How Real Is Reality TV? Essays on Representation and Truth.* Jefferson, NC: McFarland, 2006.

John Fiske — *Television Culture.* 2nd ed. New York: Routledge, 2010.

Philip Green — *Primetime Politics: The Truth About Conservative Lies, Corporate Control, and Television Culture.* Lanham, MD: Rowman & Littlefield, 2005.

Doyle Greene — *Politics and the American Television Comedy: A Critical Survey from "I Love Lucy" Through "South Park."* Jefferson, NC: McFarland, 2008.

Su Holmes and Deborah Jermyn, eds. — *Understanding Reality Television.* New York: Routledge, 2004.

Victoria E. Johnson — *Heartland TV: Prime Time Television and the Struggle for U.S. Identity.* New York: New York University Press, 2008.

Jeffrey P. Jones — *Entertaining Politics: New Political Television and Civic Culture.* Lanham, MD: Rowman & Littlefield, 2005.

Misha Kavka — *Reality Television, Affect and Intimacy.* New York: Palgrave Macmillan, 2008.

Geoff King, ed.   *The Spectacle of the Real: From Hollywood to 'Reality' TV and Beyond*. Portland, OR: Intellect, 2005.

Nicholas Laham   *Currents of Comedy on the American Screen: How Film and Television Deliver Different Laughs for Changing Times*. Jefferson, NC: McFarland, 2009.

Martha P. Largo, ed.   *The Federal Communications Commission: What Role?* New York: Nova Science, 2004.

Amanda D. Lotz   *The Television Will Be Revolutionized*. New York: New York University Press, 2007.

Jason Mittell   *Television and American Culture*. New York: Oxford University Press, 2009.

Megan Mullen   *Television in the Multichannel Age: A Brief History of Cable Television*. Malden, MA: Blackwell, 2008.

Susan Murray and Laurie Ouellette, eds.   *Reality TV: Remaking Television Culture*. New York: New York University Press, 2009.

Shelly Palmer   *Television Disrupted: The Transition from Network to Networked TV*. Boston: Focal Press, 2006.

Patrick Parsons   *Blue Skies: A History of Cable Television*. Philadelphia: Temple University Press, 2008.

Tom Reichert, ed.   *Investigating the Use of Sex in Media Promotion and Advertising.* Binghamton, NY: Best Business Books, 2007.

Kate Schuster   *Is Television a Bad Influence?* Chicago: Heinemann, 2008.

David S. Silverman   *You Can't Air That: Four Cases of Controversy and Censorship in American Television Programming.* Syracuse, NY: Syracuse University Press, 2007.

Julie Anne Taddeo and Ken Dvorak, eds.   *The Tube Has Spoken: Reality TV and History.* Lexington: University Press of Kentucky, 2010.

Ethan Thompson   *Parody and Taste in Postwar American Television Culture.* New York: Routledge, 2010.

Judith Thumim   *Inventing Television Culture: Men, Women, and the Box.* New York: Oxford University Press, 2004.

Graeme Turner and Jinna Tay, eds.   *Television Studies After TV: Understanding Television in the Post-broadcast Era.* New York: Routledge, 2009.

Index